CLASSIC KNITS *for* KIDS

Debbie Bliss

Classic Knits *for* Kids

30 Traditional Aran and Guernsey Designs for 0-6 Years

Trafalgar Square Publishing

This book is dedicated to Lynda, my sister,
and John, Edward, David and Robert.

First published in the United States of America in 1994 by
Trafalgar Square Publishing, North Pomfret, Vermont 05053

First paperback edition 1995
Reprinted 1997
First published in Great Britain in 1994 by Anaya Publishers Ltd, London

Printed and bound in Hong Kong by Dai Nippon

Editor: Alison Leach
Art Director: Carole Perks
Photography: Pia Tryde
Stylist: Marie Willey
Charts: Stephen Dew & Delia Ellimann
Pattern Checker: Tina Egleton

3 5 7 9 8 6 4 2

ISBN 1-57076-026-8

Library of Congress Catalog Card Number: 95-60033

The Publishers would like to thank Bananas, 46 Bourne Street, London SW1;
Hennes, Regent Street, London W1 and branches; Nipper, 19 Kensington Gardens,
Brighton; The Nursery Children's Shop, 103 Bishop's Road, London SW6 and The
Palace Pier, Brighton.

Typeset by Bookworm Typesetting, Manchester
Colour reproduction by J. Film Process, Singapore

Contents

INTRODUCTION

I have always loved the intricate stitch patterns and simple styles of Arans and Guernseys and was delighted to be given the opportunity to design a range of children's handknits that took its inspiration from them.

I have used the traditional stitches in a variety of designs, some classic, but where possible I have tried to give them a fresh look by working them into more contemporary styles and adding fashion details such as a shoulder-hugging collar on an Aran coat or a lacy edging on a delicate cardigan.

The collection of designs relies on texture rather than shade for its effect, and ranges from Aran fishing shirts in faded denim yarn to cabled jackets in tweed and casual cotton tops. I have also tried to keep the more inexperienced knitter in mind by including some simple shapes and styles.

The designs cover an age range from 0-6 years, but as always I have given generous allowances on the sizings as I think that children should feel comfortable and unrestricted in what they wear. All the patterns quote actual measurements so that knitters can choose to knit up whichever size they prefer.

Debbie Bliss

THE
KIDS

Duffel Coat
see page 43

Tweed
Waistcoat and
Beret
see page 44

Baby's Coat
with Beret
see page 46

Garter Stitch
Jacket
with Hat
and Bootees
see page 48

Windcheater
and Hat
see page 49

Ribbed Tunic
Style Sweater
see page 51

Longline Aran
Cardigan
see page 54

Aran Coat
see page 52

Longline Aran
Cardigan
see page 54

Aran
Fishing Shirt
see page 55

Diamond
and Bobbles
Sweater
see page 57

Striped
Pirates Hat
see page 56

Black Aran
Jacket with
Beanie Hat
see page 58

Jacket with
Sailor Collar
and Pockets
see page 59

Boxy Jacket
with Collar
see page 60

Moss Stitch
and
Garter Stitch
Guernsey
see page 62

Hearts
and Flowers
Sweater
see page 63

Hearts
and Flowers
Sweater
see page 63

Aran Cardigan with
Lace Edging
see page 65

Bobbles
and Waves
Sweater
with Bag
see page 67

Tree of Life
Guernsey
see page 69

Cotton
Aran
Sweater
see page 70

Diamond
and Moss Stitch
Cardigan
see page 72

"Star" Sweater
with Sandals
see page 73

Simple Guernsey
Style Sweater

Wee Willie Winkie Hat
see page 75

Striped Tunic Top
see page 76

Sampler
Sweater
see page 77

Aran Sweater with
Sailor Collar and
Striped Inset
see page 78

THE
KNITS

Basic Information

STANDARD ABBREVIATIONS

alt = alternate; **beg** = begin(ning); **cm** = centimetre(s); **cont** = continue; **dec** = decreas(e)ing; **foll** = following; **g** = grams; **inc** = increas(e)ing; **in** = inch(es); **K** = knit; **M1** = make one by picking up loop lying between st just worked and next st and work into the back of it; **mm** = millimetres; **patt** = pattern; **P** = purl; **psso** = pass slipped st over; **rem** = remain(ing); **rep** = repeat; **skpo** = slip 1, K1, pass slipped st over; **sl** = slip; **st(s)** = stitch(es); **st st** = stocking stitch; **tbl** = through back of loop(s); **tog** = together; yb = yarn back (ybk); **yf** = yarn forward (yfwd); **yon** = yarn over needle (yo); **yrn** = yarn round needle.

NOTES

Figures for larger sizes are given in ( ) brackets. Where only one figure appears, this applies to all sizes.

Work figures given in [ ] brackets the number of times stated afterwards, or the resultant number of stitches.

Where 0 appears no stitches or rows are worked for this size.

The yarn amounts given in the instructions are based on average requirements and should therefore be considered approximate. It is always best to use the yarn recommended in the instructions. Addresses for Rowan Yarns are given on page 80. If you want to use a substitute yarn, choose a yarn of the same type and weight as the one recommended. The following descriptions of the various Rowan yarns are meant as a guide to the yarn weight and type (i.e. cotton, mohair, wool, etcetera). Remember that the description of the yarn weight is only a rough guide and you should always test a yarn first to see if it will achieve the correct tension (gauge).

Cotton Glace: a lightweight cotton yarn (100% cotton) approx 112m/123yd per 50g/1¾oz ball
Designer DK: a double knitting (US worsted) weight yarn (100% pure new wool) approx 115m/125yd per 50g/1¾oz ball
Donegal Lambswool Tweed: a 4-ply (US sport) weight yarn (100% pure new wool) approx 100m/109yd per 30g/1oz hank
Handknit DK Cotton: a medium weight cotton yarn (100% cotton) approx 85m/90yd per 50g/1¾oz ball
Wool and Cotton: a 4-ply (US sport) weight yarn (50% superfine botany wool/50% Egyptian cotton) approx 120m/131yd per 40g/1½oz ball

The amount of a substitute yarn needed is determined by the number of metres (yards) required rather than by the number of grams (ounces). If you are unsure when choosing a suitable substitute, ask your yarn shop to advise you.

TENSION

Each pattern in this book specifies tension – the number of stitches and rows per centimetre (inch) that should be obtained on the given needles, yarn and stitch pattern. Check your tension carefully before commencing work.

Use the same yarn, needles and stitch pattern as those to be used for main work and knit a sample at least 12.5 x 12.5cm/5in square. Smooth out the finished sample on a flat surface but do not stretch it. To check the tension, place a ruler horizontally on the sample and mark 10cm/4in across with pins. Count the number of stitches between the pins. To check the row tension, place the ruler vertically on the sample and mark out 10cm/4in with pins. Count the number of rows between the pins. If the number of stitches and rows is greater than specified, try again using larger needles; if less, use smaller needles.

The stitch tension is the most important element to get right.

The following terms may be unfamiliar to US readers:

UK terms	US terms
Aran wool	*"fisherman" (unbleached wool) yarn*
ball band	*yarn wrapper*
cast off	*bind off*
DK wool	*knitting worsted yarn*
double crochet stitch	*single crochet stitch*
4-ply wool	*sport yarn*
make up (garment)	*finish (garment)*
rib	*ribbing*
saddle (on a sleeve)	*shoulder shaping*
stocking stitch	*stockinette stitch*
tension	*gauge*
waistcoat	*vest*
windcheater	*parka*

In the US balls or hanks of yarn are sold in ounces, not grams; the weights of the relevant Rowan Yarns are given on this page.

In addition, a few specific knitting and crochet terms may be unfamiliar to some readers. The list on this page explains the abbreviations used in this book to help the reader understand how to follow the various stitches and stages.

IMPORTANT

With the exception of Rowan DK Fox Tweed and Chunky, and Magpie Aran, all the yarns featured in this collection of designs are machine-washable on a wool cycle (40°C/104°F).

After washing, pat garments into shape and dry flat away from direct heat.

Rowan Den-M-nit Indigo Cotton DK will shrink and fade when it is washed, just like a pair of jeans. Unlike many 'denim look' yarns this uses real indigo dye which only coats the surface of the yarn, leaving a white core that is gradually exposed through washing and wearing.

When washed for the first time the yarn will shrink by up to one-fifth on length; the width, however, will remain the same. All the necessary adjustments have been made in the instructions for the patterns specially designed for Den-M-nit.

The knitted pieces should be washed separately at a temperature of 60-70°C (140-158°F) before sewing the garment together. The pieces can then be tumble-dried. Dye loss will be greatest during the initial wash; the appearance of the garment will, however, be greatly enhanced with additional washing and wearing.

Duffel Coat page 10

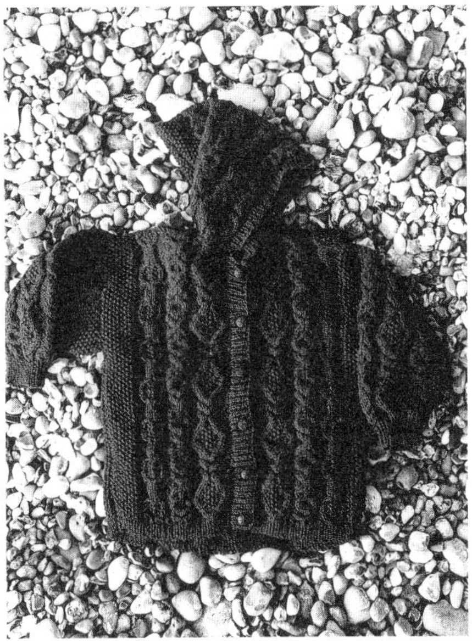

MATERIALS
9(9:10) 100g hanks of Rowan Magpie Aran.
Pair each of 4mm (No 8/US 6) and 5mm (No 6/US 8) knitting needles.
Cable needle.
6 buttons.

MEASUREMENTS

To fit age	2–3	3–4	5–6 years
Actual chest measurement	82 32¼	88 34½	96 cm 37¾in
Length	44 17¼	48 19	52 cm 20½in
Sleeve seam	27 10¾	29 11¼	31 cm 12½in

TENSION
17 sts and 25 rows to 10cm/4in square over st st on 5mm (No 6/US 8) needles.

ABBREVIATIONS
C3B = sl next st onto cable needle and leave at back of work, K2, then K st from cable needle;
C3F = sl next 2 sts onto cable needle and leave at front of work, K1, then K2 from cable needle;
C4B = sl next 2 sts onto cable needle and leave at back of work, K2, then K2 from cable needle;
C4F = sl next 2 sts onto cable needle and leave at front of work, K2, then K2 from cable needle;
Cr3L = sl next 2 sts onto cable needle and leave at front of work, P1, then K2 from cable needle;
Cr3R = sl next st onto cable needle and leave at back of work, K2, then P st from cable needle.
Also see page 42.

PANEL A
Worked over 12 sts.
1st row (right side): P4, K4, P4.
2nd row: K4, P4, K4.
3rd row: P2, sl next 3 sts onto cable needle and leave at back of work, K1, then P1, K1, P1 sts from cable needle, sl next st onto cable needle and leave at front of work, K1, P1, K1, then K st from cable needle, P2.
4th row: K2, [P1, K1] 3 times, P2, K2.
5th row: P2, [K1, P1] 3 times, K2, P2.
6th to 9th rows: Rep 4th and 5th rows twice.
10th row: K2, with yarn at front, sl next st, [K1, P1] 3 times, with yarn at front, sl next st, K2.
11th row: P2, slip next st onto cable needle and leave at front of work, P2, K1, then K st from cable needle, slip next 3 sts onto cable needle and leave at back of work, K1, then K1, P2 sts from cable needle, P2.
12th row: As 2nd row.
13th to 16th rows: Rep 1st and 2nd rows twice.
These 16 rows form patt.

PANEL B
Worked over 10 sts.
1st row (right side): P1, K8, P1.
2nd row: K1, P8, K1.
3rd row: P1, C4B, C4F, P1.
4th row: As 2nd row.
5th to 8th rows: Work 1st to 4th rows.
9th and 10th rows: As 1st and 2nd rows.
11th row: P1, C4F, C4B, P1.
12th row: K1, P8, K1.
13th to 16th rows: Work 9th to 12th rows.
These 16 rows form patt.

PANEL C
Worked over 14 sts.
1st row (right side): P3, K8, P3.
2nd row: K3, P8, K3.
3rd row: P4, C3B, Cr3L, P4.
4th row: K4, P3, K1, P2, K4.
5th row: P3, Cr3R, K1, P1, C3F, P3.
6th row: K3, P2, K1, P1, K1, P3, K3.
7th row: P2, C3B, [P1, K1] twice, Cr3L, P2.
8th row: K2, P3, K1, [P1, K1] twice, P2, K2.
9th row: P1, Cr3R, [K1, P1] 3 times, C3F, P1.
10th row: K1, P2, K1, [P1, K1] 3 times, P3, K1.
11th row: P1, Cr3L, [K1, P1] 3 times, Cr3R, P1.
12th row: As 8th row.
13th row: P2, Cr3L, [P1, K1] twice, Cr3R, P2.
14th row: As 6th row.
15th row: P3, Cr3L, K1, P1, Cr3R, P3.
16th row: As 4th row.
17th row: P4, Cr3L, Cr3R, P4.
18th row: K5, P4, K5.
19th row: P3, C4B, C4F, P3.
20th row: K3, P8, K3.
21st and 22nd rows: As 1st and 2nd rows.
23rd and 24th rows: As 19th and 20th rows.
These 24 rows form patt.

BACK
With 4mm (No 8/US 6) needles cast on 90(94:100) sts.
Work 6 rows in K1, P1 rib inc 6(6:8) sts evenly across last row [96(100:108) sts].
Change to 5mm (No 6/US 8) needles.
Work patt as follows:
1st row (right side): K1, [P1, K1] 3(4:6) times, work 1st row of Panel A, then Panel B, [work 1st row of Panel C, then Panel B]

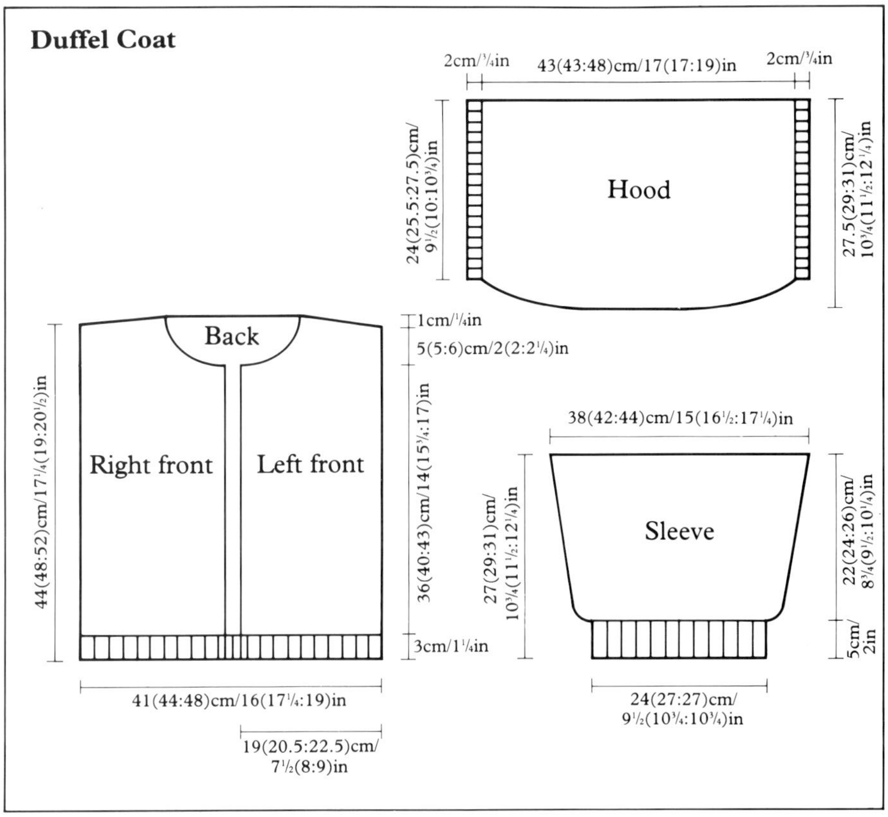

Duffel Coat
2cm/¾in
43(43:48)cm/17(17:19)in
2cm/¾in
24(25.5:27.5)cm/ 9½(10:10¾)in
Hood
27.5(29:31)cm/ 10¾(11½:12¼)in
1cm/¼in
5(5:6)cm/2(2:2¼)in
Back
44(48:52)cm/17¼(19:20½)in
Right front
Left front
36(40:43)cm/14(15¾:17)in
3cm/1¼in
41(44:48)cm/16(17¼:19)in
19(20.5:22.5)cm/ 7½(8:9)in
38(42:44)cm/15(16½:17¼)in
27(29:31)cm/ 10¾(11½:12¼)in
Sleeve
22(24:26)cm/ 8¾(9½:10¼)in
5cm/ 2in
24(27:27)cm/ 9½(10¾:10¾)in

twice, work 1st row of Panel A, K1, [P1, K1] 3(4:6) times.
This row sets position of Panels and forms moss st patt at side edges. Cont in patt as set until work measures 44(48:52)cm/ 17¼(19:20½)in from beg, ending with a wrong side row.
Shape Shoulders
Cast off 17(17:19) sts at beg of next 2 rows and 16(17:18) sts at beg of foll 2 rows. Cast off rem 30(32:34) sts working [K2 tog] twice over each cable.

LEFT FRONT
With 4mm (No 8/US 6) needles cast on 40(42:46) sts.
Work 6 rows in K1, P1 rib inc 4 sts evenly across last row [44(46:50) sts].
Change to 5mm (No 6/US 8) needles.
Work patt as follows:
1st row (right side): K1, [P1, K1] 3(4:6) times, work 1st row of Panel A, Panel B, then Panel C, P1.
2nd row: K1, work 2nd row of Panel C, Panel B, then Panel A, K1, [P1, K1] 3(4:6) times.
These 2 rows set position of Panels and form moss st patt at side edge. Cont in patt as set until Front measures 39(43:46)cm/ 15¼(17:18¼)in from beg, ending at front edge.
Shape Neck
Keeping patt correct, cast off 6 sts at beg of next row. Dec 1 st at neck edge on every row until 33(34:37) sts rem. Cont straight until Front matches Back to shoulder shaping, ending at side edge.
Shape Shoulder
Cast off 17(17:19) sts at beg of next row. Work 1 row. Cast off rem 16(17:18) sts.

RIGHT FRONT
Work as given for Left Front, working patt as follows:
1st row (right side): P1, work 1st row of Panel C, Panel B, then Panel A, K1, [P1, K1] 3(4:6) times.
2nd row: K1, [P1, K1] 3(4:6) times, work 2nd row of Panel A, Panel B, then Panel C, K1.
These 2 rows set position of Panels and form moss st patt at side edge.

SLEEVES
With 4mm (No 8/US 6) needles cast on 34(36:38) sts.
Work 5cm/2in in K1, P1 rib.
Inc row: Inc in each of first 2(4:2) sts, [rib 1, inc in each of next 3(3:2) sts] to end [60(64:64) sts].
Change to 5mm (No 6/US 8) needles.
Work patt as follows:
1st row: K1, [P1, K1] 0(1:1) time, work 1st row of Panel B, [work 1st row of Panel C, then Panel B] twice, K1, [P1, K1] 0(1:1) time.
This row sets position of Panels and form moss st patt at side edges. Cont in patt as set, inc 1 st at each end of every foll 4th row until there are 84(90:94) sts, working inc sts into moss st patt. Cont straight until Sleeve measures 27(29:31)cm/10¾ (11½:12¼)in from beg, ending with a wrong side row. Cast off.

HOOD
With 4mm (No 8/US 6) needles cast on 40(42:44) sts.
Work 3 rows in K1, P1 rib.
Inc row: Rib 0(2:0), [inc in next st, rib 1] to end [60(62:66) sts].
Change to 5mm (No 6/US 8) needles.
Work patt as follows:
1st row (right side): K1, [P1, K1] 0(1:3)

times, [work 1st(1st:11th) row of Panel B, then work 1st(1st:19th) row of Panel C] twice, work 1st(1st:11th) row of Panel B, P1.
2nd row: K1, work 2nd(2nd:12th) row of Panel B, [work 2nd(2nd:20th) row of Panel C, then work 2nd(2nd:12th) row of Panel B] twice, K1, [P1, K1] 0(1:3) times.
These 2 rows set position of Panels and form moss st patt at back edge.
Cont in patt as set, inc 1 st at end of 5th row and 6 foll 6th rows, working inc sts into moss st patt [67(69:73) sts].
Patt 28(28:40) rows straight.
Dec 1 st at beg of next row and 6 foll 6th rows [60(62:66) sts].
Patt 5 rows straight.
Change to 4mm (No 8/US 6) needles.
Dec row: [K1, P1] 0(1:0) time, [K1, P2 tog] to end [40(42:44)sts].
Work 3 rows in K1, P1 rib. Cast off in rib.

HOOD EDGING
With 4mm (No 8/US 6) needles and right side facing, pick up and K81(81:89) sts evenly along straight front edge of hood.
Next row: P1, [K1, P1] to end.
Next row: K1, [P1, K1] to end.

Rep last 2 rows once, then work first of the 2 rows again. Cast off in rib.

BUTTONHOLE BAND
With 4mm (No 8/US 6) needles and right side facing, pick up and K77(83:91) sts evenly along straight front edge of Right Front. Work 3 rows in rib as given for Hood Edging.
1st buttonhole row: Rib 2(3:2), [cast off 2, rib 11(12:14) sts more] 5 times, cast off 2, rib to end.
2nd buttonhole row: Rib to end casting on 2 sts over those cast off in previous row. Rib 2 rows. Cast off in rib.

BUTTON BAND
Work to match Buttonhole Band omitting buttonholes.

TO MAKE UP
Join shoulder seams. Fold hood in half lengthwise and join back seam. Beginning and ending at centre of front bands, sew hood in place. Sew on sleeves, placing centre of sleeves to shoulder seams. Join side and sleeve seams. Sew on buttons

Tweed Waistcoat and Beret page 11

MATERIALS
Waistcoat: 6 50g hanks of Rowan DK Fox Tweed.
Pair of 4mm (No 8/US 6) knitting needles.
Cable needle.
12 buttons.
Beret: 2 50g hanks of Rowan DK Fox Tweed.
Pair each of 3¼mm (No 10/US 3) and 4mm (No 8/US 6) knitting needles.

MEASUREMENTS

To fit age	2-4 years
Actual chest measurement	80 cm 31½in
Length	43 cm 17 in

TENSION
25 sts and 34 rows to 10cm/4in square over pattern on 4mm (No 8/US 6) needles.

ABBREVIATIONS
C6F = sl next 3 sts onto cable needle and leave at front of work, K3, then K3 from cable needle.
Also see page 42.

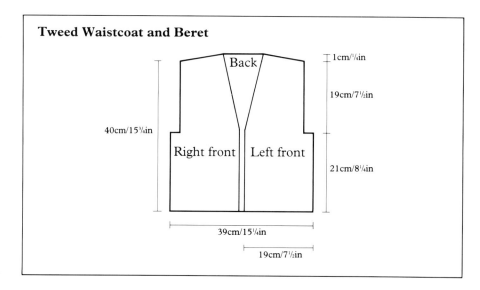

Tweed Waistcoat and Beret
Back
Right front
Left front
1cm/¼in
19cm/7½in
21cm/8¼in
40cm/15¾in
39cm/15¼in
19cm/7½in

WAISTCOAT

BACK
With 4mm (No 8/US 6) needles cast on 97 sts.
Work patt as follows:
1st row (right side): P1, [K1, P1] 3 times, * K6, P1, [K1, P1] twice; rep from * to last 13 sts, K6, P1, [K1, P1] 3 times.
2nd row: P1, [K1, P1] 3 times, * P7, [K1, P1] twice; rep from * to last 13 sts, P7, [K1, P1] 3 times.
3rd and 4th rows: As 1st and 2nd rows.
5th row: P1, [K1, P1] 3 times, * C6F, P1, [K1, P1] twice; rep from * to last 13 sts, C6F, P1, [K1, P1] 3 times.
6th row: As 2nd row.
7th and 8th row: As 1st and 2nd rows.
These 8 rows form patt. Cont in patt until Back measures 21cm/8¼in from beg, ending with a wrong side row.
Shape Armholes
Cast off 5 sts at beg of next 2 rows [87 sts].
Cont straight in patt until Back measures 40cm/15¾in from beg, ending with a wrong side row.
Shape Shoulders
Cast off 13 sts at beg of next 2 rows and 12 sts at beg of foll 2 rows.
Cast off rem 37 sts.

LEFT FRONT
With 4mm (No 8/US 6) needles cast on 34 sts.
Work patt as follows:
1st row (right side): P1, [K1, P1] 3 times, * K6, P1, [K1, P1] twice; rep from * once more, K5.
2nd row: Cast on 2 sts, P7, *[P1, K1] twice, P7; rep from * once more, P1, [K1, P1] 3 times.
3rd row: P1, [K1, P1] 3 times, * K6, P1, [K1, P1] twice; rep from * once more, K6, inc in last st.
4th row: Cast on 2 sts, K1, P1, K1, P7, * [P1, K1] twice, P7; rep from * once more, P1, [K1, P1] 3 times.
5th row: P1, [K1, P1] 3 times, *C6F, P1, [K1, P1] twice; rep from * once more, C6F, P1, K1, P1, inc in last st.
6th row: Cast on 2 sts, P2, * [P1, K1] twice, P7; rep from * twice more, P1, [K1, P1] 3 times.
7th row: P1, [K1, P1] 3 times, * K6, P1, [K1, P1] twice; rep from * twice more, K1, inc in last st.
8th row: Inc in first st, P2, * [P1, K1] twice, P7; rep from * twice more, P1, [K1, P1] 3 times.
9th row: P1, [K1, P1] 3 times, * K6, P1, [K1, P1] twice; rep from * twice more, K3, inc in last st.
10th row: Inc in first st, P4, * [P1, K1] twice, P7; rep from * twice more, P1, [K1, P1] 3 times.
11th row: P1, [K1, P1] 3 times, * K6, P1, [K1, P1] twice; rep from * twice more, K5, inc in last st [47 sts].
12th row: P7, * [P1, K1] twice, P7; rep from * twice more, P1, [K1, P1] 3 times.
13th row: P1, [K1, P1] 3 times, *C6F, P1, [K1, P1] twice; rep from * twice more, C6F, P1.
The last 2 rows set position of patt. Cont in patt as set until Front measures 21cm/8¼in from beg, ending at side edge.
Shape Armhole
Cast off 5 sts at beg of next row [42 sts].
Patt 1 row.
Shape Neck
Keeping patt correct, dec 1 st at neck edge on next row and every foll 3rd row until 25 sts rem. Cont straight until Front matches

Back to shoulder shaping, ending at armhole edge.
Shape Shoulder
Cast off 13 sts at beg of next row. Work 1 row. Cast off rem 12 sts.

RIGHT FRONT
With 4mm (No 8/US 6) needles cast on 34 sts.
Work patt as follows:
1st row (right side): K5, * [P1, K1] twice, P1, K6; rep from * once more, P1, [K1, P1] 3 times.
2nd row: P1, [K1, P1] 3 times, * P7, [K1, P1] twice; rep from * once more, P4, inc in last st.
3rd row: Cast on 2 sts, K1, P1, K6, * [P1, K1] twice, P1, K6; rep from * once more, P1, [K1, P1] 3 times.
4th row: P1, [K1, P1] 3 times, * P7, [K1, P1] twice; rep from * once more, P7, inc in last st.
5th row: Cast on 2 sts, * [P1, K1] twice, P1, C6F; rep from * twice more, P1, [K1, P1] 3 times.
6th row: P1, [K1, P1] 3 times, * P7, [K1, P1] twice; rep from * once more, P7, K1, P1, K1, inc in last st.
7th row: Cast on 2 sts, K3, * [P1, K1] twice, P1, K6; rep from * twice more, P1, [K1, P1] 3 times.
8th row: P1, [K1, P1] 3 times, * P7, [K1, P1] twice; rep from * twice more, P2, inc in last st.
9th row: Inc in first st, K3, * [P1, K1] twice, P1, K6; rep from * twice more, P1, [K1, P1] 3 times.
10th row: P1, [K1, P1] 3 times, * P7, [K1, P1] twice, more, P4, inc in last st.
11th row: Inc in first st, K5, * [P1, K1] twice, P1, K6; rep from * twice more, P1, [K1, P1] 3 times [47 sts].
12th row: P1, [K1, P1] 3 times, * P7, [K1, P1] twice; rep from * twice more, P7.
13th row: P1, C6F, * [P1, K1] twice, P1, C6F; rep from * twice more, P1, [K1, P1] 3 times.
The last 2 rows set position of patt.
Complete to match Left Front.

FLAPS (make 2)
With 4mm (No 8/US 6) needles cast on 21 sts.
Work patt as follows:
1st row: K1, [P1, K1] to end.
This row forms moss st patt. Cont in patt until Flap measures 3cm/1¼in from beg.
Dec 1 st at each end of every row until 3 sts rem.
Next row: Sl 1, K2 tog, psso and fasten off.

SIDE BELTS (make 2)
With 4mm (No 8/US 6) needles cast on 7 sts.
Work 9cm/3½in in moss st patt as given for Flaps. Dec 1 st at each end of next 2 rows.
Next row: Sl 1, K2 tog, psso and fasten off.

ARMBANDS
Join shoulder seams.
With 4mm (No 8/US 6) needles and right side facing, pick up and K71 sts evenly around armhole edge. Work 7 rows in moss st patt as given for Flaps. Cast off in patt.

BACK WELT
With 4mm (No 8/US 6) needles cast on 7 sts. Work in moss st patt as given for Flaps until band, when slightly stretched, fits along lower edge of Back. Cast off.

BUTTON BAND AND COLLAR
With 4mm (No 8/US 6) needles cast on 7 sts.
Work in moss st patt as given for Flaps until band fits along cast on edge of Left Front, easing band round lower shaped edge and up straight edge to beg of neck shaping.
Shape Collar
Cont in moss st, inc 1 st at beg of next row and at same edge on every foll 3rd row until there are 17 sts, ending at straight edge.
Cast off 7 sts at beg of next row. Work 1 row. Cast on 7 sts at beg of next row. Inc 1 st at beg of next row and at same edge on 3 foll 3rd rows [21 sts]. Cont straight until shaped edge of Collar fits up front neck edge and along to centre back neck. Cast off in patt.
Sew band and collar in place.
Mark band along straight front edge to indicate position of 4 buttons: first one 1cm/¼in up from end of lower edge shaping, last one 1cm/¼in down from beg of neck shaping and rem 2 evenly spaced between.

BUTTONHOLE BAND AND COLLAR
Work as given for Button Band and Collar reversing shapings and making buttonholes at markers as follows:
1st buttonhole row (right side): Moss st 2, cast off 3, moss st to end.
2nd row: Moss st 2, cast on 3, moss st to end.

TO MAKE UP
Sew buttonhole band and collar in place, then join back seam of collar. Sew on back welt. Join row ends of armbands to cast off sts at armholes. Join side seams. Sew on flaps as shown in photograph and secure point in place with button. Attach slightly stretched side belts at sides, then sew on button at each end of each belt. Sew on buttons to left front band and one to each lapel.

BERET

TO MAKE

With 3¼mm (No 10/US 3) needles cast on 96 sts.

Work 7 rows in K1, P1 rib.

Inc row: Rib 3, M1, rib 3, [M1, rib 2, M1, rib 3] to end [133 sts].

Change to 4mm (No 8/US 6) needles.

1st row: K1, [P1, K1] to end.

This row forms moss st patt. Cont in patt until work measures 11cm/4¼in from beg.

Shape Top

Dec row: [Moss st 19, P3 tog] to last st, moss st 1.

Moss st 1 row.

Dec row: [Moss st 17, P3 tog] to last st, moss st 1.

Moss st 1 row.

Dec row: [Moss st 15, P3 tog] to last st, moss st 1.

Cont in this way, dec 12 sts as set on every alt row until 13 sts rem.

Break off yarn, thread end through rem sts, pull up and secure.

Join seam.

Baby's Coat with Beret page 12

MATERIALS

Coat: 5 50g hanks of Rowan DK Fox Tweed.

Pair of 4mm (No 8/US 6) knitting needles.

Cable needle.

Medium size crochet hook.

10 buttons.

Beret: 2 50g hanks of Rowan DK Fox Tweed.

Pair of 4mm (No 8/US 6) knitting needles.

Cable needle.

MEASUREMENTS

To fit age	1 year
Actual chest measurement	60 cm 23½in
Length	30 cm 11¾in
Sleeve seam	20 cm 8 in

TENSION

25 sts and 34 rows to 10cm/4in square over patt on 4mm (No 8/US 6) needles.

ABBREVIATIONS

C4F = sl next 2 sts onto cable needle and leave at front of work, K2, then K2 from cable needle;

C6F = sl next 3 sts onto cable needle and leave at front of work, K3, then K3 from cable needle.

Also see page 42.

COAT

BACK

With 4mm (No 8/US 6) needles cast on 75 sts.

Work patt as follows:

1st row (right side): P1, [K1, P1] 3 times, * K6, P1, [K1, P1] twice; rep from * to last 13 sts, K6, P1, [K1, P1] 3 times.

2nd row: P1, [K1, P1] 3 times, * P7, [K1, P1] twice; rep from * to last 13 sts, P7, [K1, P1] 3 times.

3rd and 4th rows: As 1st and 2nd rows.

5th row: P1, [K1, P1] 3 times, * C6F, P1, [K1, P1] twice; rep from * to last 13 sts, C6F, P1, [K1, P1] 3 times.

6th row: As 2nd row.

7th and 8th rows: As 1st and 2nd rows.

These 8 rows form patt. Cont in patt until Back measures 30cm/11¾in from beg, ending with a wrong side row.

Shape Shoulders

Cast off 11 sts at beg of next 2 rows and 12 sts at beg of foll 2 rows. Cast off rem 29 sts.

POCKET LININGS (make 2)

With 4mm (No 8/US 6) needles cast on 18 sts.

Work patt as follows:

1st row: [K1, P1] 3 times, K6, [P1, K1] 3 times.

2nd row: [K1, P1] 3 times, P6, [P1, K1] 3 times.

3rd and 4th rows: As 1st and 2nd rows.

5th row: [K1, P1] 3 times, C6F, [P1, K1] 3 times.

6th row: As 2nd row.

7th and 8th rows: As 1st and 2nd rows.

These 8 rows form patt. Patt a further 17 rows. Leave these sts on a holder.

LEFT FRONT

With 4mm (No 8/US 6) needles cast on 40 sts.

Work patt as follows:

1st row (right side): P1, [K1, P1] 3 times, * K6, P1, [K1, P1] twice; rep from * to end.

2nd row: * [P1, K1] twice, P7; rep from * to last 7 sts, [P1, K1] 3 times, P1.

3rd and 4th rows: As 1st and 2nd rows.

5th row: P1, [K1, P1] 3 times, * C6F, P1, [K1, P1] twice; rep from * to end.

6th row: As 2nd row.

7th and 8th rows: As 1st and 2nd rows.

These 8 rows form patt. Patt a further 16 rows.

Place Pocket

Next row: Patt 12, cast off next 18 sts, patt to end.

Next row: Patt 10, patt across sts of first pocket lining, patt to end.

Cont in patt across all sts until Front measures 19cm/7½in from beg, ending with a wrong side row.

Shape Neck

Keeping patt correct, dec 1 st at front edge on next row and every foll alt row until 23 sts rem. Cont straight until Front matches Back to shoulder shaping, ending at side edge.

Shape Shoulder

Cast off 11 sts at beg of next row. Work 1 row. Cast off rem 12 sts.

Mark front edge to indicate 4 buttons: first one 10 rows up from cast on edge, last one 4 rows below beg of neck shaping and rem 2 evenly spaced between.

RIGHT FRONT
With 4mm (No 8/US 6) needles cast on 40 sts.
Work patt as follows:
1st row (right side): * P1, [K1, P1] twice, K6; rep from * to last 7 sts, P1, [K1, P1] 3 times.
2nd row: P1, [K1, P1] 3 times, * P7, [K1, P1] twice; rep from * to end.
3rd and 4th rows: As 1st and 2nd rows.
5th row: * P1, [K1, P1] twice, C6F; rep from * to last 7 sts, P1, [K1, P1] 3 times.
6th row: As 2nd row.
7th and 8th rows: As 1st and 2nd rows.
These 8 rows form patt. Patt a further 2 rows.
Buttonhole row: Patt 2, yf, skpo, patt to end.
Patt a further 13 rows.
Place Pocket
Next row: Patt 10, cast off next 18 sts, patt to end.
Next row: Patt 12, patt across sts of second pocket lining, patt to end.
Complete to match Left Front, working buttonhole at markers as before.

SLEEVES
With 4mm (No 8/US 6) needles cast on 38 sts.
Work patt as follows:
1st row (right side): P1, [K1, P1] twice, * K6, P1, [K1, P1] twice; rep from * to end.
2nd row: P1, [K1, P1] twice, * P7, [K1, P1] twice; rep from * to end.
These 2 rows set patt. Cont in patt as set, inc 1 st at each end of next row and every foll 6th row until there are 58 sts, working inc sts into patt. Cont straight until Sleeve measures 20cm/8in from beg, ending with a wrong side row. Cast off.

COLLAR AND LAPELS
With 4mm (No 8/US 6) needles cast on 17 sts for Left Front Lapel.
1st row: K1, [P1, K1] to end.
This row forms moss st patt. Cont in moss st, dec 1 st at end of next row and at same edge on foll 11 rows [5 sts]. Leave these sts on a holder.
With 4mm (No 8/US 6) needles cast on 53 sts for centre of Collar.
Work 15 rows in moss st. Leave these sts on a spare needle.
With 4mm (No 8/US 6) needles cast on 17 sts for Right Front Lapel.
Work 1 row in moss st. Cont in moss st, dec 1 st at beg of next row and at same edge on foll 11 rows [5 sts].
Next row: Work 2 tog, patt 3, cast on 1 st, then patt across sts of centre of Collar, cast on 1 st, patt 3, work 2 tog across sts of Left Front Lapel [63 sts].

Work a further 5 rows, dec 1 st at each end of every row. Cast off in patt.

SIDE BELTS (make 2)
With 4mm (No 8/US 6) needles cast on 5 sts. Work 11cm/4¼in in moss st as given for Collar and Lapels. Cast off in patt.

TO MAKE UP
Join shoulder seams. Sew cast off edge of collar and lapels to neck edge.
Sew on sleeves, placing centre of sleeves to shoulder seams. Join side and sleeve seams.
Crochet edging: With crochet hook and right side facing, work 1 row of double crochet along cast on edge of back, right front, along front edge then around right lapel, collar and left lapel, down front edge of left front and cast on edge, slip stitch in first double crochet. Do not turn. Now work 1 row of backward double crochet (double crochet worked from left to right), slip stitch in first double crochet. Fasten off. Work crochet edgings around lower edge of sleeves and along pocket tops.
Catch down pocket linings. Attach slightly stretched side belts at sides, then sew button at each end of each belt. Sew on buttons to left front and one to each lapel.

BERET
TO MAKE
With 4mm (No 8/US 6) needles cast on 73 sts.
1st row: K1, [P1, K1] to end.
This row forms moss st patt. Work a further 6 rows in moss st.
Inc row: Inc in first st, moss st 3, * [M1, moss st 1] 3 times, moss st 2, work 3 times in next st, moss st 3; rep from * to last 6 sts, [M1, moss st 1] 3 times, moss st 2, work twice in last st [113 sts].
Work patt as follows:
1st row (right side): [Moss st 4, K6, moss st 4] to last st, moss st 1.
2nd row: Moss st 1, [moss st 4, P6, moss st 4] to end.
3rd (inc) row: [Moss st 4, M1, K6, M1, moss st 4] to last st, moss st 1.
4th row: Moss st 1, [moss st 5, P6, moss st 5] to end.
5th (inc) row: [Moss st 5, M1, C6F, M1, moss st 5] to last st, moss st 1.
6th row: Moss st 1, [moss st 6, P6, moss st 6] to end.
7th (inc) row: [Moss st 6, M1, K6, M1, moss st 6] to last st, moss st 1.
8th row: Moss st 1, [moss st 7, P6, moss st 7] to end.
These 8 rows set patt.
Inc row: [Patt 7, M1, patt 6, M1, patt 7] to last st, patt 1.
Patt 3 rows straight.

Inc row: [Patt 8, M1, patt 6, M1, patt 8] to last st, patt 1.
Patt 3 rows straight.
Inc row: [Patt 9, M1, patt 6, M1, patt 9] to last st, patt 1 [209 sts].
Patt 9 rows straight.
Dec row: [Patt 8, work 2 tog, patt 6, work 2 tog tbl, patt 8] to last st, patt 1.
Patt 3 rows straight.
Dec row: [Patt 7, work 2 tog, patt 6, work 2 tog tbl, patt 7] to last st, patt 1.
Patt 3 rows straight.
Dec row: [Patt 6, work 2 tog, patt 6, work 2 tog tbl, patt 6] to last st, patt 1.
Cont in this way, dec 16 sts as set on every foll 4th row until 97 sts rem.
Patt 3 rows straight.
Dec row: [Patt 3, K2 tog, K2, K2 tog tbl, patt 3] to last st, patt 1.
Next row: Patt 1, [patt 3, P4, patt 3] to end.
Next row: Patt 1, [patt 3, C4F, patt 3] to last st, patt 1.
Next row: Patt 1, [patt 3, P4, patt 3] to end.
Dec row: [Patt 1, work 2 tog, K4, work 2 tog tbl, patt 1] to last st, patt 1.
Next row: Patt 1, [patt 2, P4, patt 2] to end.
Next row: Patt 1, [patt 2, C4F, patt 2] to last st, patt 1.
Next row: Patt 1, [patt 2, P4, patt 2] to end.
Dec row: [Work 2 tog, K4, work 2 tog tbl] to last st, patt 1.
Next row: Patt 1, [patt 1, P4, patt 1] to end.
Dec row: Patt 1, [C4F, P2 tog] to end.
P 1 row.
Dec row: P1, [K2 tog, K2 tog tbl, P1] to end.
Dec row: P1, [P2 tog] to end.
Break off yarn, thread end through rem 13 sts, pull up and secure. Join seam.

Baby's Coat with Beret

Back

Right front

Left front

30cm/11¾in

30cm/11¾in

16cm/6¼in

1cm/½in

11cm/4¼in

19cm/7½in

20cm/8in

23cm/9in

Sleeve

15cm/6in

Garter Stitch Jacket with Hat and Bootees page 13

MATERIALS
Jacket: 4(5:5) 50g hanks of Rowan DK Fox Tweed (MC).
5 buttons.
Hat: 1(2:2) 50g hanks of Rowan DK Fox Tweed (MC).
Bootees: 1 50g hank of Rowan DK Fox Tweed (MC).
All items: 1 50g ball of Rowan Designer DK Wool (A) for embroidery.
Pair of 3¾mm (No 9/US 5) knitting needles.

MEASUREMENTS

To fit age	6	9	12 months
Actual chest measurement	62 24½	64 25	66 cm 26 in
Length	27 10¾	30 11¾	33 cm 13 in
Sleeve seam (with cuff turn back)	16 6¼	18 7	20 cm 8 in

TENSION
20 sts and 44 rows to 10cm/4in square over garter st (every row K) on 3¾mm (No 9/US 5) needles using MC.

ABBREVIATIONS
See page 42.

JACKET
BACK
With MC cast on 62(64:66) sts.
Work in garter st until Back measures 27(30:33)cm/10¾(11¾:13)in from beg.
Shape Shoulders
Cast off 9(9:10) sts at beg of next 2 rows and 10 sts at beg of foll 2 rows. Cast off rem 24(26:26) sts.

POCKET LININGS (make 2)
With MC cast on 18(19:20) sts. Work 26(28:30) rows in garter st.
Leave these sts on a holder.

LEFT FRONT
With MC cast on 34(35:36) sts. Work 30(32:34) rows in garter st.
Place Pocket
Next row: K8, cast off next 18(19:20) sts, K to end.
Next row: K8, K across sts of pocket lining, K to end.
Cont in garter st until Front measures 24(27:30)cm/9½(10½:11¾)in from beg, ending at front edge.
Shape Neck
Cast off 7(8:8) sts at beg of next row. Dec 1 st at neck edge on every row until 19(19:20) sts rem. Cont straight for a few rows until Front matches Back to shoulder shaping, ending at side edge.
Shape Shoulder
Cast off 9(9:10) sts at beg of next row. Work 1 row. Cast off rem 10 sts.
Mark front edge to indicate 5 buttons: first one 2cm/¾in up from cast on edge, last one 1cm/¾in down from cast off edge of neck and rem 3 evenly spaced between.

RIGHT FRONT
Work as given for Left Front, working buttonholes at markers as follows:
1st buttonhole row (right side): K2, cast off 2, K to end.
2nd buttonhole row: K to last 2 sts, cast on 2, K to end.

SLEEVES
With MC cast on 32(38:42) sts. Work 38(40:42) rows in garter st for cuff.
Cont in garter st, inc 1 st at each end of next row and every foll 5th(6th:6th) row until there are 50(52:54) sts. Cont straight until Sleeve measures 21(23:25)cm/8¼(9:10)in from beg. Cast off.

TO MAKE UP
Join shoulder seams. Sew on sleeves, placing centre of sleeves to shoulder seams. Join side and sleeve seams, reversing seams on cuffs. Catch down pocket linings. With A, work blanket st along pocket tops, lower edges of back and fronts, front edges of fronts and around neck edge. Work blanket st with A along lower edges of sleeves. Turn back cuffs. Sew on buttons.

HAT
EAR FLAPS (make 2)
With MC cast on 8(9:10) sts. Work in garter st, inc 1 st at each end of 4 foll alt rows [16(17:18) sts]. Work 10(12:12) rows straight.
Dec 1 st at each end of next row and foll 4th row.
Inc 1 st at each end of 4th row and 2 foll 3rd rows [18(19:20) sts].
Work 1 row. Leave these sts on a holder.

MAIN PART
With MC cast on 9(10:11) sts, K across sts of first ear flap, cast on 30(32:34) sts, K across sts of second ear flap, cast on 9(10:11) sts [84(90:96) sts]. Work 43(45:47) rows in garter st.
Shape Top
1st row: * K19(8:4), K2 tog; rep from * to last 21(0:6) sts, K to end [81 sts].
Work 3 rows straight.
5th row: [K7, K2 tog] to end.
Work 3 rows straight.
9th row: [K6, K2 tog] to end.
Work 3 rows straight.
13th row: [K5, K2 tog] to end.
Work 3 rows straight.
17th row: [K4, K2 tog] to end.
Work 3 rows straight.
21st row: [K2, K2 tog] to last st, K1 [34 sts].
22nd row and 5 foll alt rows: K.
23rd row: [K6, sl 1, K1, psso, K1, K2 tog, K6] twice.
25th row: [K5, sl 1, K1, psso, K1, K2 tog, K5] twice.
27th row: [K4, sl 1, K1, psso, K1, K2 tog, K4] twice.
29th row: [K3, sl 1, K1, psso, K1, K2 tog, K3] twice.
31st row: [K2, sl 1, K1, psso, K1, K2 tog, K2] twice.
33rd row: [K1, sl 1, K1, psso, K1, K2 tog, K1] twice.
Work 3 rows straight.

Garter Stitch Jacket with Hat and Bootees

Back

Right front — Left front

27(30:33)cm/10¾(11¾:13)in

24(27:30)cm/9½(10½:11¾)in

1cm/¼in
3cm/1¼in

31(32:33)cm/12¼(12½:13)in

17(17.5:18)cm/6¾(7:7¼)in

25(26:27)cm/10(10¼:10½)in

Sleeve

16(18:20)cm/6¼(7:8)in

21(23:25)cm/8¼(9:10)in

16(19:21)cm/6¼(7½:8¼)in

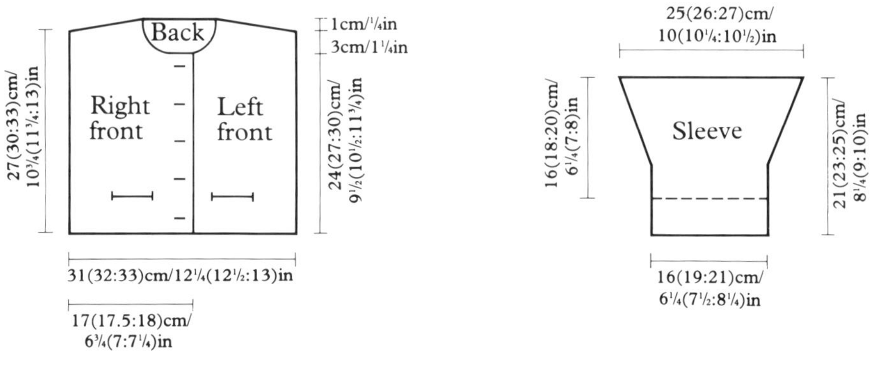

37th row: [Sl 1, K1, psso, K1, K2 tog] twice.
K 1 row.
Break off yarn, thread end through rem 6 sts, pull up and secure.

TO MAKE UP
Join back seam. With A, work blanket st along lower edge of main part and around ear flaps.

BOOTEES
TO MAKE
With MC cast on 30(33:36) sts. Work 31 rows in garter st.
Shape Instep
Next row: K20(22:24), turn.
Next row: K10(11:12), turn.
Work 20(22:24) rows in garter st on centre 10(11:12) sts for instep.
Break off yarn.
With right side facing, rejoin yarn at base of instep and pick up and K10(11:12) sts along side edge of instep, K across centre 10(11:12) sts, then pick up and K10(11:12) sts along other side edge of instep, K rem 10(11:12) sts [50(55:60) sts]. Work 6 rows in garter st.
Next row (wrong side): [Pick up st 5 rows below corresponding with next st on left hand needle and K them tog] to end. Work 8(10:10) rows in garter st. Break off yarn.
Shape Sole
Next row: Slip first 20(22:24) sts onto right hand needle, rejoin yarn and K10(11:12) sts, turn.
Next row: K9(10:11), K2 tog, turn.
Rep last row until 10(11:12) sts rem.
Next row: K0(1:0), [K2 tog] to end.
Cast off rem 5(6:6) sts.
Join back seam, reversing seam on top 3cm/1¼in for cuff. With A, work blanket st around cast on edge. Turn back cuff.
Make one more.

Windcheater and Hat page 14

MATERIALS
Windcheater: 5 100g hanks of Rowan Magpie Aran Tweed.
Hat: 1 100g hank of Rowan Magpie Aran Tweed.
Pair each of 4mm (No 8/US 6) and 5mm (No 6/US 8) knitting needles. Cable needle and 6 buttons for Windcheater.

MEASUREMENTS

To fit age	3 years
Actual chest measurement	86 cm 33¾in
Length	42 cm 16½in
Sleeve seam	24 cm 9½in

TENSION
17 sts and 25 rows to 10cm/4in square over st st on 5mm (No 6/US 8) needles.

ABBREVIATIONS
C4B = sl next 2 sts onto cable needle and leave at back of work, K2, then K2 from cable needle;
C4F = sl next 2 sts onto cable needle and leave at front of work, K2, then K2 from cable needle;
Cr3L = sl next 2 sts onto cable needle and leave at front of work, P1, then K2 from cable needle;
Cr3R = sl next st onto cable needle and leave at back of work, K2, then P st from cable needle;
MB = make bobble as follows: [K1, P1, K1, P1] all in next st, turn, P4, turn, K4, then pass 2nd, 3rd and 4th sts over first st.
Also see page 42.

WINDCHEATER
PANEL A
Worked over 20 sts.
1st row (right side): K4, P2, K8, P2, K4.
2nd row and 2 foll alt rows: P4, K2, P8, K2, P4.
3rd row: [C4F, P2, C4B] twice.
5th row: As 1st row.
7th row: C4F, P2, C4F, C4B, P2, C4B.
8th row: As 2nd row.
These 8 rows form patt.

PANEL B
Worked over 15 sts.
1st row (right side): P2, K3, [P1, K1] 3 times, K2, P2.
2nd row: K2, P2, [K1, P1] 3 times, K1, P2, K2.
3rd row: P2, Cr3L, P1, [K1, P1] twice, Cr3R, P2.
4th row: K3, P3, [K1, P1] twice, P2, K3.
5th row: P3, Cr3L, K1, P1, K1, Cr3R, P3.
6th row: K4, P2, K1, P1, K1, P2, K4.
7th row: P4, Cr3L, P1, Cr3R, P4.
8th row: K5, P5, K5.
9th row: P5, K2, MB, K2, P5.
10th row: As 8th row.
11th row: P5, MB, K3, MB, P5.
12th to 14th rows: As 8th to 10th rows.
15th row: P4, Cr3R, P1, Cr3L, P4.
16th row: As 6th row.
17th row: P3, Cr3R, K1, P1, K1, Cr3L, P3.
18th row: As 4th row.
19th row: P2, Cr3R, P1, [K1, P1] twice, Cr3L, P2.
20th row: As 2nd row.
These 20 rows form patt.

BACK
With 4mm (No 8/US 6) needles cast on 73 sts.
1st row: K1, [P1, K1] to end.
This row forms moss st patt. Cont in moss st patt until work measures 3cm/1¼in from beg.
**** Inc row:** Patt 4, * inc in each of next 2 sts, patt 2, [inc in next st, patt 1] 3 times, patt 1, inc in each of next 2 sts, patt 2, inc in next st, patt 7, inc in next st, patt 2; rep from * once, inc in each of next 2 sts, patt 2, [inc in next st, patt 1] 3 times, patt 1, inc in each of next 2 sts, patt 4 [98 sts]. ****
Change to 5mm (No 6/US 8) needles.
Work main patt as follows:
1st row (right side): Moss st 3, P1, [work 1st row of Panel A, then Panel B] twice, work 1st row of Panel A, P1, moss st 3.
2nd row: Moss st 3, K1, [work 2nd row of Panel A, then Panel B] twice, work 2nd row of Panel A, K1, moss st 3.
These 2 rows set position of Panels. Cont in patt as set until work measures 13cm/5in from beg, ending with a right side row.
Dec row: Patt 4, * [work 2 tog] twice, patt 2, [work 2 tog, patt 1] 3 times, patt 1, [work 2 tog] twice, patt 2, work 2 tog, patt 7, work 2 tog, patt 2; rep from * once, [work 2 tog] twice, patt 2, [work 2 tog, patt 1] 3 times, patt 1, [work 2 tog] twice, patt 4 [73 sts].
Change to 4mm (No 8/US 6) needles.
Work in rib as follows:
Next row (right side): K1, [P1, K1] to end.
Next row: P1, [K1, P1] to end.
Rep last 2 rows 3 times more, then work 1st of the 2 rows again.

49

Work from ** to **.
Change to 5mm (No 6/US 8) needles.
Cont in main patt as set before until Back measures 42cm/16½in from beg, ending with a wrong side row.
Shape Shoulders
Cast off 32 sts at beg of next 2 rows. Cast off rem 34 sts.

LEFT FRONT
With 4mm (No 8/US 6) needles cast on 35 sts.
Work 3cm/1¼in in moss st patt as given for Back.
*** **Inc row:** [Patt 3, inc in next st] twice, patt 7, inc in next st, patt 2, inc in each of next 2 sts, patt 2, [inc in next st, patt 1] 3 times, patt 1, inc in each of next 2 sts, patt 4 [45 sts]. ***
Change to 5mm (No 6/US 8) needles.
Work main patt as follows:
1st row (right side): Moss st 3, P1, work 1st row of Panel A, then Panel B, K4, P2.
2nd row: K2, P4, work 2nd row of Panel B, then Panel A, K1, moss st 3.
3rd row: Moss st 3, P1, work 3rd row of Panel A, then Panel B, C4F, P2.
4th row: K2, P4, work 4th row of Panel B, then Panel A, K1, moss st 3.
These 4 rows set position of Panels. Cont in patt as set until Front measures 13cm/5in from beg, ending with a right side row.
Dec row: [Patt 3, work 2 tog] twice, patt 7, work 2 tog, patt 2, [work 2 tog] twice, patt 2, [work 2 tog, patt 1] 3 times, patt 1, [work 2 tog] twice, patt 4 [35 sts].
Change to 4mm (No 8/US 6) needles.
Work 9 rows in rib as given for Back, then work from *** to ***.
Change to 5mm (No 6/US 8) needles.
Cont in main patt as set before until Front measures 37cm/14½in from beg, ending at front edge.
Shape Neck
Keeping patt correct, cast off 6 sts at beg of next row. Dec 1 st at neck edge on every row until 32 sts rem. Cont straight until Front matches Back to shoulder shaping, ending at side edge. Cast off.

RIGHT FRONT
With 4mm (No 8/US 6) needles cast on 35 sts.
Work 3cm/1¼in in moss st patt as given for Back.
**** **Inc row:** Patt 4, inc in each of next 2 sts, patt 2, [inc in next st, patt 1] 3 times, patt 1, inc in each of next 2 sts, patt 2, inc in next st, patt 7, [inc in next st, patt 3] twice [45 sts]. ****
Change to 5mm (No 6/US 8) needles.
Work main patt as follows:
1st row (right side): P2, K4, work 1st row of Panel B, then Panel A, P1, moss st 3.
2nd row: Moss st 3, K1, work 2nd row of Panel A, then Panel B, P4, K2.
3rd row: P2, C4B, work 3rd row of Panel B, then Panel A, P1, moss st 3.
4th row: Moss st 3, K1, work 4th row of Panel A, then Panel B, P4, K2.
These 4 rows set position of Panels. Cont in patt as set until Front measures 13cm/5in from beg, ending with a right side row.
Dec row: Patt 4, [work 2 tog] twice, patt 2, [work 2 tog, patt 1] 3 times, patt 1, [work 2 tog] twice, patt 2, work 2 tog, patt 7, [work 2 tog, patt 3] twice [35 sts].
Change to 4mm (No 8/US 6) needles.
Work 9 rows in rib as given for Back, then work from **** to ****.
Change to 5mm (No 6/US 8) needles.
Cont in main patt as set before and complete to match Left Front.

SLEEVES
With 4mm (No 8/US 6) needles cast on 35 sts.
Work 4cm/1½in in rib as given for Back, ending with a right side row.
Inc row: Rib 1, * inc in each of next 2 sts, rib 1, inc in each of next 5 sts, rib 1, inc in each of next 2 sts *; rib 2, inc 3 times in next st, rib 5, work 3 times in next st, rib 2, rep from * to * once, rib 1 [57 sts].
Change to 5mm (No 6/US 8) needles.
Work main patt as follows:
1st row (right side): P1, work 1st row of Panel A, Panel B, then Panel A, P1.
2nd row: K1, work 2nd row of Panel A, Panel B, then Panel A, K1.
These 2 rows set position of Panels. Cont in patt as set, inc 1 st at each end of next row and every foll 3rd row until there are 81 sts, working inc sts into moss st.
Cont straight until Sleeve measures 24cm/9½in from beg, ending with a wrong side row. Cast off.

BUTTON BAND
With 4mm (No 8/US 6) needles cast on 7 sts.
Work in moss st patt as given for Back until band when slightly stretched, fits up front edge of Left Front. Cast off. Sew band in place.

Mark band to indicate buttons: first one 1cm/¼in up from cast on edge, last one 1cm/¼in down from cast off edge and rem 4 evenly spaced between.

BUTTONHOLE BAND
Work to match Button Band making buttonholes at markers as follows:
1st buttonhole row (right side): Patt 2, cast off 2, patt to end.
2nd buttonhole row: Patt 3, cast on 2, patt to end.
Sew band in place.

COLLAR
Join shoulder seams.
With 4mm (No 8/US 6) needles, right side facing and beg at centre of buttonhole band, pick up and K20 sts up right front neck, 25 sts across back neck and 20 sts down left front neck to centre of button band [65 sts].
1st row: K1, [P1, K1] to end.
2nd row: P1, K1, P1, [P1, K1] to last 4 sts, P2, K1, P1.
3rd row: K1, P1, K1, M1, [P1, K1] to last 4 sts, P1, M1, K1, P1, K1.
4th row: P1, [K1, P1] to end.
5th row: K1, P1, K1, M1, [K1, P1] to last 4 sts, K1, M1, K1, P1, K1.
Rep 2nd to 5th rows 3 times more, then work 2nd to 4th rows again.
Cast off loosely in patt.

TO MAKE UP
Sew on sleeves, placing centre of sleeves to shoulder seams. Join side and sleeve seams. Sew on buttons.

HAT
With 5mm (No 6/US 8) needles cast on 92 sts.
Work 9cm/3½in in K1, P1 rib.
Work patt as follows:
1st row (right side): P1, * [K1, P1] 7 times, K1; rep from * to last st, P1.
2nd row: K1, * [K1, P1] 6 times, P1, K1, P1; rep from * to last st, K1.
These 2 rows form patt. Cont in patt for a further 4cm/1½in, ending with a wrong side row.
Shape Crown
Dec row: P1, * K1, P1, yb, sl 1 purlwise, K1, psso, patt 11; rep from * to last st, P1.
Patt 3 rows.
Dec row: P1, * K1, P1, yb, sl 1 purlwise, K1, psso, patt 10; rep from * to last st, P1.
Patt 3 rows.
Dec row: P1, * K1, P1, yb, sl 1 purlwise, K1, psso, patt 9; rep from * to last st, P1.
Cont in this way, dec 6 sts as set on every foll alt row until 26 sts rem, ending with a wrong side row.
Dec row: P1, * K1, P1, yb, sl 1 purlwise, K1, psso; rep from * to last st, P1.
Next row: K1, * P1, K1, P1; rep from * to last st, K1.
Dec row: P1, K1, * P1, yb, sl 1 purlwise, K1, psso; rep from * to end.
Next row: * P1, K1; rep from * to end.
Dec row: P1, yb, * sl 1 purlwise, K1, psso; rep from * to last st, P1.
Break off yarn, thread end through rem 8 sts, pull up and secure. Join back seam, reversing seam on rib section for brim. Turn back brim.

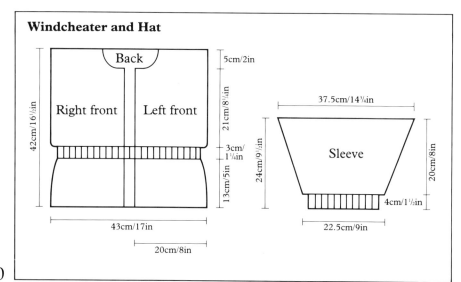

Windcheater and Hat

Back

Right front   Left front

42cm/16½in

5cm/2in

21cm/8¼in

3cm/1¼in

13cm/5in

24cm/9½in

37.5cm/14¼in

Sleeve

20cm/8in

4cm/1½in

43cm/17in

20cm/8in

22.5cm/9in

Ribbed Tunic Style Sweater page 15

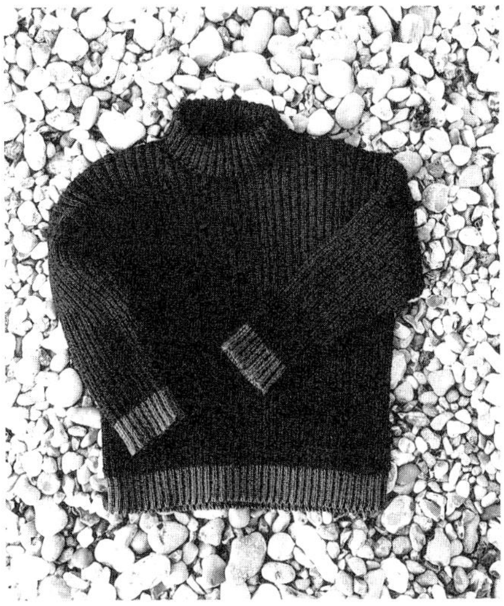

MATERIALS
9(10) 50g balls of Rowan Designer DK Wool in Black (MC).
1(2) 50g balls of same in Rust (A).
Pair each of 3¼mm (No 10/US 3) and 4mm (No 8/US 6) knitting needles.

MEASUREMENTS

To fit age	2–4	4–6 years
Actual chest measurement	81 32	90 cm 35½in
Length	45 17¾	50 cm 19¾in
Sleeve seam	25 10	31 cm 12¼in

TENSION
36 sts and 30 rows to 10cm/4in square over rib pattern on 4mm (No 8/US 6) needles.

ABBREVIATIONS
See page 42.

BACK
With 3¼mm (No 10/US 3) needles and A, cast on 146(162) sts.
1st row (right side): K2, [P2, K2] to end.
2nd row: P2, [K2, P2] to end.
These 2 rows form rib patt. Cont in patt until Back measures 4(5)cm/1½(2)in from beg, ending with a wrong side row.
Change to 4mm (No 8/US 6) needles and MC.
Cont in patt until Back measures 45(50)cm/17¾(19¾)in from beg, ending with a wrong side row.
Shape Shoulders
Cast off 24(27) sts at beg of next 4 rows.
Leave rem 50(54) sts on a holder.

FRONT
Work as given for Back until Front measures 40(44)cm/15¾(17½)in from beg, ending with a wrong side row.
Shape Neck
Next row: Patt 58(64), turn.
Work on this set of sts only. Dec 1 st at neck edge on every row until 48(54) sts rem. Cont straight until Front matches Back to shoulder shaping, ending at side edge.
Shape Shoulders
Cast off 24(27) sts at beg of next row.
Work 1 row. Cast off rem 24(27) sts.
With right side facing, slip centre 30(34) sts onto a holder, rejoin yarn to rem sts and patt to end. Complete to match first side.

SLEEVES
With 3¼mm (No 10/US 3) needles and A, cast on 66(70) sts.
Work 4(5)cm/1½(2)in in rib as given for Back, ending with a wrong side row.
Change to 4mm (No 8/US 6) needles and MC.
Cont in patt, inc 1 st at each end of every alt row until there are 96(84) sts, then on every foll 3rd row until there are 108(116) sts, working inc sts into patt. Cont straight until Sleeve measures 25(31)cm/10(12¼)in from beg, ending with a wrong side row.
Cast off.

COLLAR
Join right shoulder seam.
With 3¼mm (No 10/US 3) needles, MC and right side facing, pick up and K18 sts down left front neck, rib across centre front sts, pick up and K16(20) sts up right front neck, then rib back neck sts [114(126) sts].
Cont in rib across all sts for 12cm/4¾in.
Cast off loosely in rib.

TO MAKE UP
Join left shoulder and collar seam, reversing seam on last 6cm/2¼in. Sew on sleeves, placing centre of sleeves to shoulder seams. Join side and sleeve seams.

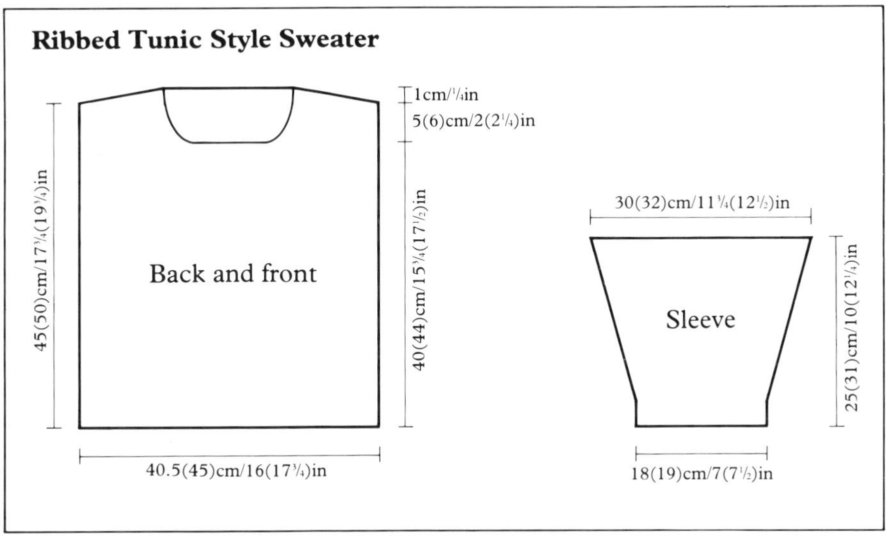
Ribbed Tunic Style Sweater
1cm/¼in
5(6)cm/2(2¼)in
45(50)cm/17¾(19¾)in
40(44)cm/15¾(17½)in
Back and front
40.5(45)cm/16(17¾)in
30(32)cm/11¾(12½)in
Sleeve
25(31)cm/10(12¼)in
18(19)cm/7(7½)in

Aran Coat page 18

MATERIALS
8 100g hanks of Rowan Magpie Aran.
Pair each of 4mm (No 8/US 6) and
5mm (No 6/US 8) knitting needles.
One 4mm (No 8/US 6) circular knitting
needle.
Cable needle.
7 buttons.

MEASUREMENTS

To fit age	4–6 years
Actual chest measurement	93 cm 36½in
Length	52 cm 20½in
Sleeve seam	29 cm 11½in

TENSION
17 sts and 25 rows to 10cm/4in square
over st st on 5mm (No 6/US 8) needles.

ABBREVIATIONS
Cr4L = sl next 3 sts onto cable needle
and leave at front of work, K1, then K1
tbl, P1, K1 tbl sts from cable needle;
Cr4R = sl next st onto cable needle and
leave at back of work, K1 tbl, P1, K1 tbl,
then K st from cable needle;
Tw4L = sl next 3 sts onto cable needle
and leave at front of work, P1, then K1,
P1, K1 sts from cable needle;
Tw4R = sl next st onto cable needle and
leave at back of work, K1, P1, K1, then
P st from cable needle;
MB = make bobble as follows: [K1, yf,
K1, yf, K1] all in next st, turn, P5, turn,
sl 2, K3 tog, pass 2 slipped sts over.
Also see page 42.

PANEL A
Worked over 14 sts.
1st row (right side): K1 tbl, P3, slip next
3 sts onto cable needle and leave at front of
work, K1, P1, K1, then K1, P1, K1 sts
from cable needle, P3, K1 tbl.
2nd row: P1, K3, P1, K1, P2, K1, P1, K3,
P1.
3rd row: K1 tbl, P3, K1, P1, K2, P1, K1,
P3, K1 tbl.
4th row: As 2nd row.
5th and 6th rows: As 1st and 2nd rows.
7th row: K1 tbl, P2, Tw4R, Tw4L, P2,
K1 tbl.
8th row: P1, K2, [P1, K1, P1, K2] twice,
P1.
9th row: K1 tbl, P2, [K1, P1, K1, P2]
twice, K1 tbl.
10th row: As 8th row.
11th to 16th rows: Rep 9th and 10th rows
3 times.
17th row: K1 tbl, P2, Tw4L, Tw4R, P2,
K1 tbl.
18th row: As 2nd row.
These 18 rows form patt.

PANEL B
Worked over 23 sts.
1st row (right side): P7, Cr4R, K1 tbl,
Cr4L, P7.
2nd row: K7, P1, [K1, P1] 4 times, K7.
3rd row: P6, Cr4R, K1, K1 tbl, K1, Cr4L,
P6.
4th row: K6, P1, K1, P1, [K2, P1] twice,
K1, P1, K6.
5th row: P5, Cr4R, K2, K1 tbl, K2, Cr4L,
P5.
6th row: K5, P1, K1, P2, K2, P1, K2, P2,
K1, P1, K5.
7th row: P4, Cr4R, K1 tbl, [K2, K1 tbl]
twice, Cr4L, P4.
8th row: K4, P1, [K1, P1] twice, [K2, P1]
twice, [K1, P1] twice, K4.
9th row: P3, Cr4R, K1, K1 tbl, [K2, K1
tbl] twice, K1, Cr4L, P3.
10th row: K3, P1, K1, P1, [K2, P1] 4
times, K1, P1, K3.
11th row: P2, Cr4R, K2, [K1 tbl, K2] 3
times, Cr4L, P2.
12th row: K2, P1, K1, P1, K3, P1, [K2,
P1] twice, K3, P1, K1, P1, K2.
13th row: P2, K1 tbl, P1, K1 tbl, K3, MB,
[K2, MB] twice, K3, K1 tbl, P1, K1 tbl,
P2.
14th row: K2, P1, K1, P1, K3, Pl tbl, [K2,
P1 tbl] twice, K3, P1, K1, P1, K2.
15th row: P2, K1 tbl, P1, K1 tbl, P3, K1
tbl, P1, K3 tbl, P1, K1 tbl, P3, K1 tbl, P1,
K1 tbl, P2.
16th row: K8, P1, K1, P3, K1, P1, K8.
These 16 rows form patt.

PANEL C
Worked over 14 sts.
1st row (right side): K1 tbl, P3, slip next
3 sts onto cable needle and leave at back of
work, K1, P1, K1, then K1, P1, K1 sts
from cable needle, P3, K1 tbl.
2nd row: P1, K3, P1, K1, P2, K1, P1, K3,
P1.
3rd row: K1 tbl, P3, K1, P1, K2, P1, K1,
P3, K1 tbl.
4th row: As 2nd row.
5th and 6th rows: As 1st and 2nd rows.
7th row: K1 tbl, P2, Tw4R, Tw4L, P2,
K1 tbl.
8th row: P1, K2, [P1, K1, P1, K2] twice,
P1.
9th row: K1 tbl, P2, [K1, P1, K1, P2]
twice, K1 tbl.
10th row: As 8th row.
11th to 16th rows: Rep 9th and 10th rows
3 times.
17th row: K1 tbl, P2, Tw4L, Tw4R, P2,
K1 tbl.
18th row: As 2nd row.
These 18 rows form patt.

PANEL D
Worked over 6 sts.
1st row (right side): P1, K4, P1.
2nd row: K1, P4, K1.
3rd row: P1, slip next 2 sts onto cable
needle and leave at front of work, K2, then
K2 from cable needle, P1.
4th row: K1, P4, K1.
These 4 rows form patt.

BACK
With 4mm (No 8/US 6) needles cast on 99
sts.
1st row (right side): K1, [P1, K1] to end.
2nd row: P1, [K1, P1] to end.
Rib 1 more row.

Aran Coat

Back

Right front Left front

52cm/20½in

36cm/14in

1cm/¼in

14cm/5½in

2cm/¼in

45cm/17¼in

23cm/9in

31cm/12¼in

Sleeve

29cm/11½in

24cm/9½in

5cm/2in

22cm/8½in

Inc row: Rib 10, * M1, rib 8, M1, rib 6, M1, rib 1, M1, rib 6, M1, rib 8, M1, rib 10 *; M1, rib 11, rep from * to * [112 sts]. Change to 5mm (No 6/US 8) needles. Work patt as follows:
1st row: P2, * work 1st row of Panel A, Panel B, then Panel C *; work 1st row of Panel D, rep from * to *, P2.
2nd row: K2, * work 2nd row of Panel C, Panel B, then Panel A *; work 2nd row of Panel D, rep from * to *, K2.
These 2 rows set position of Panels. Cont in patt as set until Back measures 52 cm/20½in from beg, ending with a wrong side row.
Shape Shoulders
Cast off 17 sts at beg of next 2 rows and 18 sts at beg of foll 2 rows. Cast off rem 42 sts.

POCKET LININGS (make 2)
With 5mm (No 6/US 8) needles cast on 19 sts.
Beg with a P row, work 31 rows in reverse st st.
Inc row: K4, M1, K5, M1, K1, M1, K5, M1, K4 [23 sts].
Work 1st to 5th rows of Panel B. Leave these sts on a holder.

LEFT FRONT
With 4mm (No 8/US 6) needles cast on 49 sts.
Work 3 rows in rib as given for Back welt.
Inc row: Rib 10, M1, rib 8, M1, rib 6, M1, rib 1, M1, rib 6, M1, rib 8, M1, rib 10 [55 sts].
Change to 5mm (No 6/US 8) needles.
Work patt as follows:
1st row: P2, work 1st row of Panel A, Panel B, then Panel C, P2.
2nd row: K2, work 2nd row of Panel C, Panel B, then Panel A, K2.
These 2 rows set position of Panels. Cont in patt as set for a further 29 rows.
Dec row: Patt 16, K2 tog, [P1, K1] 3 times, [P1, K2 tog] twice, P1, [K1, P1] 3 times, K2 tog, patt 16 [51 sts].
Next row: Patt 16, P1, [K1, P1] 9 times, patt 16.
Next row: Patt 16, K1, [P1, K1] 9 times, patt 16.
Rep last 2 rows once more.
Next row: Patt 16, cast off in rib next 19 sts, patt to end.
Place Pocket
Next row: Patt 16, patt across sts of one pocket lining, patt to end [55 sts].
Cont in patt until Front measures 38cm/15in from beg, ending with a wrong side row.
Shape neck
Keeping patt correct, dec 1 st at neck edge on next 7 rows, then on every foll alt row to 35 sts. Cont straight until Front matches Back to shoulder shaping, ending at side edge.
Shape Shoulder
Cast off 17 sts at beg of next row. Work 1 row. Cast off rem 18 sts.

RIGHT FRONT
Work as given for Left Front.

SLEEVES
With 4mm (No 8/US 6) needles cast on 37 sts.
Work 5cm/2in in rib as given for Back welt, ending with a right side row.
Inc row: Inc in first st, rib 5, [M1, rib 2] 6 times, M1, rib 1, M1, [rib 2, M1] 6 times, rib 5, inc in last st [53 sts].
Change to 5mm (No 6/US 8) needles.
Work patt as follows:
1st row: P1, work 1st row of Panel A, Panel B, then Panel C, P1.
2nd row: K1, work 2nd row of Panel C, Panel B, then Panel A, K1.
These 2 rows set position of Panels. Cont in patt as set, inc 1 st at each end of 3rd row and 4 foll 4th rows, working inc sts into Panel D patt, then on every foll 5th row until there are 75 sts, working inc sts into reverse st st. Cont straight until Sleeve measures 29cm/11½in from beg, ending with a wrong side row. Cast off.

COLLAR
Right side
With 4mm (No 8/US 6) needles cast on 4 sts.
1st row (right side): P2, K1 tbl, P1.
2nd row: K1, P1, K2.
3rd row: Cast on 3 sts, P1, K1, P3, K1 tbl, P1.
4th row: K1, P1, K3, P1, K1.
5th row: Cast on 3 sts, P1, K2, P1, K1, P3, K1 tbl, P1.
6th row: K1, P1, K3, P1, K1, P2, K1.
7th row: Cast on 3 sts, P2, K1, P1, K2, P1, K1, P3, K1 tbl, P1.
8th row: K1, P1, K3, P1, K1, P2, K1, P1, K2.
9th row: Cast on 3 sts, P1 (last st of 1st row of Panel B), work 1st row of Panel C, P1.
10th row: K1, work 2nd row of Panel C, K1 (first st of 2nd row of Panel B).
Cont as set, casting on 2 sts at beg of next row and 6 foll alt rows, then 1 st at beg of foll 6 alt rows, working extra sts into Panel B patt [36 sts]. Patt 1 row. Leave these sts on a holder.
Left Side
With 4mm (No 8/US 6) needles cast on 4 sts.
1st row (right side): P1, K1 tbl, P2.
2nd row: Cast on 3 sts, K1, P1, K3, P1, K1.
3rd row: P1, K1 tbl, P3, K1, P1.
4th row: Cast on 3 sts, K1, P2, K1, P1, K3, P1, K1.
5th row: P1, K1 tbl, P3, K1, P1, K2, P1.
6th row: Cast on 3 sts, K2, P1, K1, P2, K1, P1, K3, P1, K1.
7th row: P1, K1 tbl, P3, K1, P1, K2, P1, K1, P2.
8th row: Cast on 3 sts, K1, P1, K3, P1, K1, P2, K1, P1, K3, P1, K1.
9th row: P1, work 1st row of Panel A, P1 (first st of 1st row of Panel B).
10th row: Cast on 2 sts, K3 (last 3 sts of 2nd row of Panel B), work 2nd row of Panel A, K1.
Cont as set, casting on 2 sts at beg of 6 foll alt rows, then 1 st at beg of foll 6 alt rows, working extra sts into Panel B patt [36 sts]. Patt 2 rows.
Next row: Patt to end, cast on 38 sts, then patt across sts of right side [110 sts].
Next row: K1, * work 12th row of Panel C, work 14th row of Panel B, work 12th row of Panel A *; work 4th row of Panel D, rep from * to *, K1.
Cont in patt as set for a further 26 rows.
Next row: Patt 15, P2 tog, patt to last 17 sts, P2 tog, patt 15.

Next row: Patt 15, K2 tog, patt to last 17 sts, K2 tog, patt 15.
Rep last 2 rows twice more.
Next row: Patt 15, P3 tog, patt to last 18 sts, P3 tog, patt 15.
Next row: Patt 15, K3 tog, patt to last 18 sts, K3 tog, patt 15.
Rep last 2 rows once more.
Next row: Patt 16 and sl these sts onto a holder for left side border, cast off next 6 sts, patt to last 16 sts and sl last 16 sts onto a holder for right side border, turn.
Work on centre sts only. Cast off 6 sts at beg of next 3 rows. Cast off rem 26 sts.
With right side facing, rejoin yarn to right side border and patt to end.
Cont in patt until border fits along shaped edge of Collar to centre, ending with wrong side row. Cast off.
With wrong side facing, rejoin yarn to left side border and patt to end.
Complete to match right side border. Sew borders in place, then join them together.

COLLAR EDGING
With 4mm (No 8/US 6) circular needle and right side facing, pick up and K189 sts round outside edge of Collar. Work 3 rows in rib as given for Back welt. Cast off in rib.

BUTTONHOLE BAND
With 4mm (No 8/US 6) needles and right side facing, pick up and K79 sts along front edge of Right Front. Beg with a 2nd row, work 2 rows in rib as given for Back welt.
Buttonhole row: Rib 2, [P2 tog, yrn, rib 10] 6 times, P2 tog, yrn, rib 3.
Rib 2 rows. Cast off in rib.

BUTTON BAND
Work to match Buttonhole Band omitting buttonholes.

TO MAKE UP
Join shoulder seams. Sew on collar beginning and ending at centre of front bands. Sew on sleeves, placing centre of sleeves to shoulder seams. Catch down pocket linings. Sew on buttons.

Longline Aran Cardigan page 19

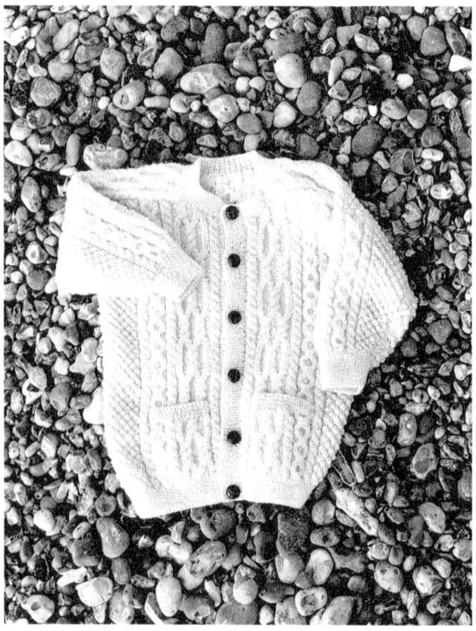

MATERIALS

10(10:11) 50g balls of Rowan Designer DK Wool.
Pair each of 3¼mm (No 10/US 3) and 4mm (No 8/US 6) knitting needles.
Cable needle.
6 buttons.

MEASUREMENTS

To fit age	2–3	4–5	6–7 years
Actual chest measurement	78 30¾	82 32¼	86 cm 33¾in
Length	45 17¾	50 19¾	55 cm 21¾in
Sleeve seam	22 8¾	24 9½	26 cm 10¼in

TENSION

24 sts and 32 rows to 10cm/4in square over st st on 4mm (No 8/US 6) needles.

ABBREVIATIONS

C4B = sl next 2 sts onto cable needle and leave at back of work, K2, then K2 from cable needle;
C4F = sl next 2 sts onto cable needle and leave at front of work, K2, then K2 from cable needle;
Cr3L = sl next 2 sts onto cable needle and leave at front of work, P1, then K2 from cable needle;
Cr3R = sl next st onto cable needle and leave at back of work, K2, then P st from cable needle.
Also see page 42.

PANEL A

Worked over 12 sts.
1st row (right side): P2, K8, P2.
2nd row and 2 foll alt rows: K2, P8, K2.
3rd row: P2, C4B, C4F, P2.
5th row: As 1st row.
7th row: P2, C4F, C4B, P2.
8th row: As 2nd row.
These 8 rows form patt.

PANEL B

Worked over 18 sts.
1st row (right side): P1, K2, P4, K4, P4, K2, P1.
2nd row: K1, P2, K4, P4, K4, P2, K1.
3rd row: P1, K2, P4, C4B, P4, K2, P1.
4th row: As 2nd row.
5th row: P1, [Cr3L, P2, Cr3R] twice, P1.
6th row: K2, [P2, K2] 4 times.
7th row: P2, [Cr3L, Cr3R, P2] twice.
8th row: K3, P4, K4, P4, K3.
9th row: P3, C4B, P4, C4B, P3.
10th row: As 8th row.
11th row: P3, K4, P4, K4, P3.
12th to 18th rows: Work 8th to 11th rows once, then work 8th to 10th rows again.
19th row: P2, [Cr3R, Cr3L, P2] twice.
20th row: As 6th row.
21st row: P1, [Cr3R, P2, Cr3L] twice, P1.
22nd to 24th rows: Work 2nd to 4th rows.
25th to 28th rows: Work 1st to 4th rows.
These 28 rows form patt.

BACK

With 3¼mm (No 10/US 3) needles cast on 105(109:113) sts.
Work 4cm/1½in in K1, P1 rib, beg alt rows P1.
Inc row: Rib 2(6:7), [inc in next st, rib 4(3:3), inc in next st, rib 4(3:2)] to last 3(7:8) sts, inc in next st, rib to end [126(134:142) sts].
Change to 4mm (No 8/US 6) needles.
Work patt as follows:
1st row (right side): P15(19:23), [K4, work 1st row of Panel A, K4, work 1st row of Panel B] twice, K4, work 1st row of Panel A, K4, P15(19:23).
2nd row: K1, * P3 tog, [K1, P1, K1] all in next st *; rep from * to * 2(3:4) times more, K2, [P4, work 2nd row of Panel A, P4, work 2nd row of Panel B] twice, P4, work 2nd row of Panel A, P4, K2, rep from * to * 3(4:5) times, K1.
3rd row: P15(19:23), C4F, work 3rd row of Panel A, C4F, work 3rd row of Panel B, C4F, work 3rd row of Panel A, C4B, work 3rd row of Panel B, C4B, work 3rd row of Panel A, C4B, P15(19:23).
4th row: K1, * [K1, P1, K1] all in next st, P3 tog *; rep from * to * 2(3:4) times more, K2, [P4, work 4th row of Panel A, P4, work 4th row of Panel B] twice, P4, work 4th row of Panel A, P4, K2, rep from * to * 3(4:5) times, K1.
These 4 rows set position of Panels and form patt at side edges. Cont in patt as set until work measures 41(46:51)cm/16(18:20)in from beg, ending with a wrong side row.

Shape Shoulders
Cast off 44(46:48) sts at beg of next 2 rows. Cast off rem 38(42:46) sts.

POCKET LININGS (make 2)

With 3¼mm (No 10/US 3) needles cast on 32 sts. Work in K1, P1 rib for 8cm/3in. Leave these sts on a holder.

LEFT FRONT

With 3¼mm (No 10/US 3) needles cast on 46(48:50) sts.
Work 4cm/1½in in K1, P1 rib.
Inc row: Rib 4(2:0), [inc in next st, rib 2] to last 6(4:2) sts, inc in next st, rib to end [59(63:67) sts].
Change to 4mm (No 8/US 6) needles.
Work patt as follows:
1st row (right side): P15(19:23), K4, work 1st row of Panel A, K4, work 1st row of Panel B, K4, P2.
2nd row: K2, P4, work 2nd row of Panel B, P4, work 2nd row of Panel A, P4, K2, * P3 tog, [K1, P1, K1] all in next st; rep from * 2(3:4) times more, K1.
3rd row: P15(19:23), C4F, work 3rd row of Panel A, C4F, work 3rd row of Panel B, C4F, P2.
4th row: K2, P4, work 4th row of Panel B, P4, work 4th row of Panel A, P4, K2, * [K1, P1, K1] all in next st, P3 tog; rep from * 2(3:4) times more, K1.
These 4 rows set position of Panels and form patt at side edge. Cont in patt as set until Front measures 12cm/4¾in from beg, ending with a wrong side row.

Place Pocket
Next row: Patt 20(24:28), sl next 32 sts onto a holder, patt across sts of first pocket lining, patt to end.
Cont in patt across all sts until Front measures 7 rows less than Back to shoulder shaping, thus ending at front edge.

Longline Aran Cardigan

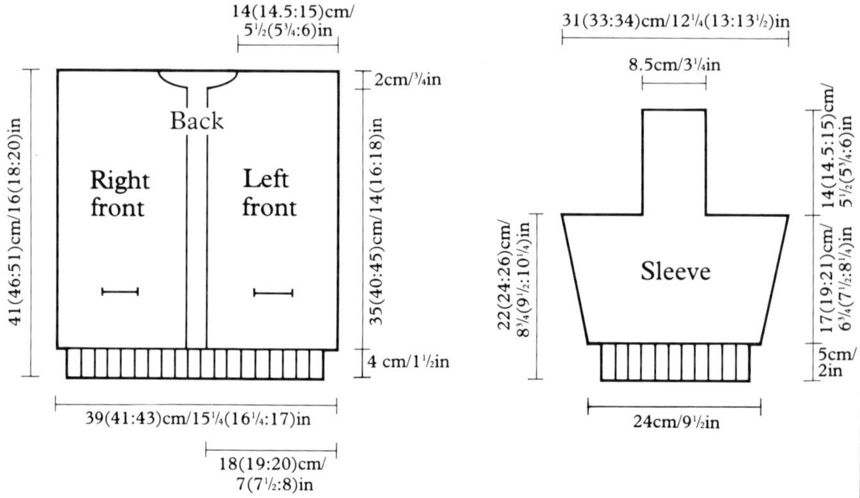
14(14.5:15)cm/
5½(5¾:6)in
2cm/¾in
Back
Right front
Left front
41(46:51)cm/16(18:20)in
35(40:45)cm/14(16:18)in
4 cm/1½in
39(41:43)cm/15¼(16¼:17)in
18(19:20)cm/
7(7½:8)in
31(33:34)cm/12¼(13:13½)in
8.5cm/3¼in
Sleeve
22(24:26)cm/
8¾(9½:10¼)in
14(14.5:15)cm/
5½(5¾:6)in
17(19:21)cm/
6¾(7½:8¼)in
5cm/
2in
24cm/9½in

Shape Neck
Keeping patt correct, cast off 8(10:12) sts at beg of next row and 3 sts at beg of foll alt row. Dec 1 st at neck edge on next 4 rows. Cast off rem 44(46:48) sts.

RIGHT FRONT
With 3¼mm (No 10/US 3) needles cast on 46(48:50) sts.
Work 4cm/1½in in K1, P1 rib.
Inc row: Rib 5(3:1), [inc in next st, rib 2] to last 5(3:1) sts, inc in next st, rib 4(2:0) [59(63:67) sts].
Change to 4mm (No 8/US 6) needles.
Work patt as follows:
1st row (right side): P2, K4, work 1st row of Panel B, K4, work 1st row of Panel A, K4, P15(19:23).
2nd row: K1, * P3 tog, [K1, P1, K1] all in next st; rep from * 2(3:4) times more, K2, P4, work 2nd row of Panel A, P4, work 2nd row of Panel B, P4, K2.
3rd row: P2, C4B, work 3rd row of Panel B, C4B, work 3rd row of Panel A, C4B, P15(19:23).
4th row: K1, * [K1, P1, K1] all in next st, P3 tog; rep from * 2(3:4) times more, K2, P4, work 4th row of Panel A, P4, work 4th row of Panel B, P4, K2.
These 4 rows set position of Panels and form patt at side edge. Cont in patt as set until Front measures 12cm/4¾in from beg, ending with a wrong side row.
Place Pocket
Next row: Patt 7, sl next 32 sts onto a holder, patt across sts of second pocket lining, patt to end.
Complete to match Left Front, reversing neck shaping.

SLEEVES
With 3¼mm (No 10/US 3) needles cast on 50 sts.
Work 5cm/2in in K1, P1 rib.
Inc row: Rib 3, [inc in each of next 2 sts, rib 1] to last 2 sts, rib 2 [80 sts].
Change to 4mm (No 8/US 6) needles.
Work patt as follows:
1st row (right side): P11, K4, work 1st row of Panel A, K4, work 1st row of Panel B, K4, work 1st row of Panel A, K4, P11.
2nd row: K1, * P3 tog, [K1, P1, K1] all in next st *; rep from * to * once more, K2, P4, work 2nd row of Panel A, P4, work 2nd row of Panel B, P4, work 2nd row of Panel A, P4, K2, rep from * to * twice, K1.
3rd row: P11, C4F, work 3rd row of Panel A, C4F, work 3rd row of Panel B, C4B, work 3rd row of Panel A, C4B, P11.
4th row: K1, * [K1, P1, K1] all in next st, P3 tog *; rep from * to * once more, K2, P4, work 4th row of Panel A, P4, work 4th row of Panel B, P4, work 4th row of Panel A, P4, K2, rep from * to * twice, K1.
These 4 rows set position of Panels and form patt at side edges.
Cont in patt as set, inc 1 st at each end of next row and every foll 3rd row until there are 102(106:110) sts, working inc sts into side edge patt. Cont straight until Sleeve measures 22(24:26)cm/8¾(9½:10¼)in from beg, ending with a wrong side row.
Shape Saddles
Cast off 36(38:40) sts at beg of next 2 rows. Cont on rem 30 sts until saddle measures 14(14.5:15)cm/5½ (5¾:6)in, ending with a wrong side row. Cast off.

NECKBAND
Join saddles to shoulders of back and front, then sew on remaining sleeve tops.
With 3¼mm (No 10/US 3) needles and right side facing, pick up and K89(97:103) sts evenly around neck edge.
1st row: P1, [K1, P1] to end.
2nd row: K1, [P1, K1] to end.
Rep last 2 rows 3 times more, then work first of the 2 rows again. Cast off in rib.

BUTTONHOLE BAND
With 3¼mm (No 10/US 3) needles and right side facing, pick up and K107(121:133) sts evenly along front edge of one front including neckband. Work in rib as given for Neckband.
1st buttonhole row: Rib 3(2:3), [cast off 2, rib 17(20:22) sts more] 5 times, cast off 2, rib to end.
2nd buttonhole row: Rib to end casting on 2 sts over those cast off in previous row. Rib 4 rows. Cast off in rib.

BUTTON BAND
Work to match Buttonhole Band omitting buttonholes.

POCKET TOPS
With 3¼mm (No 10/US 3) needles and right side facing, work in rib as given for Neckband across sts of one pocket top dec 1 st [31 sts]. Work a further 5 rows in rib. Cast off in rib.

TO MAKE UP
Join side and sleeve seams. Catch down pocket linings and sides of pocket tops. Sew on buttons.

Aran Fishing Shirt page 20

MATERIALS
10(11:12) 50g balls of Rowan Den-M-nit Indigo Cotton DK.
Pair each of 3¼mm (No 10/US 3), 4mm (No 8/US 6) and 4½mm (No 7/US 7) knitting needles.
Cable needle.

MEASUREMENTS

To fit age	2–3	3–4	4–5 years

The following measurements are after the garment has been washed to the instructions given on ball band.

	2–3	3–4	4–5
Actual chest measurement	72 28¼	76 30	80 cm 31½in
Length	42 16½	45 17¼	48 cm 19 in
Sleeve seam	24 9½	26 10¼	28 cm 11 in

TENSION
20 sts and 34 rows to 10cm/4in square over double moss stitch pattern on 4½mm (No 7/US 7) needles after washing.

ABBREVIATIONS
C4B = sl next 2 sts onto cable needle and leave at back of work, K2, then K2 from cable needle;
C4F = sl next 2 sts onto cable needle and leave at front of work, K2, then K2 from cable needle;
Cr3L = sl next 2 sts onto cable needle and leave at front of work, P1, then K2 from cable needle;
Cr3R = sl next st onto cable needle and leave at back of work, K2, then P st from cable needle.
Also see page 42.

PANEL A
Worked over 22 sts.
1st row (right side): P4, K2, P3, K4, P3, K2, P4.
2nd row: K4, P2, K3, P4, K3, P2, K4.
3rd row: P3, Cr3R, P2, Cr3R, Cr3L, P2, Cr3L, P3.
4th row: [K3, P2] twice, K2, [P2, K3] twice.
5th row: [P2, Cr3R] twice, P2, [Cr3L, P2] twice.
6th row: K2, P2, K3, P2, K4, P2, K3, P2, K2.
7th row: P1, [Cr3R, P2] twice, make bobble as follows: pick up loop lying between st just worked and next st and work K1, P1, K1 into it, turn, P3, turn, K3, turn, P1, P2 tog, turn, K2 tog, P next st, then pass bobble st over the P st, P1, Cr3L, P2, Cr3L, P1.
8th row: K1, P2, K3, P2, K6, P2, K3, P2, K1.
9th row: P1, [Cr3L, P2] twice, [P2, Cr3R] twice, P1.
10th row: As 6th row.
11th row: [P2, Cr3L] twice, P2, [Cr2R, P2] twice.
12th row: As 4th row.
13th row: P3, Cr3L, P2, Cr3L, Cr3R, P2, Cr3R, P3.
14th row: As 2nd row.
Rows 3rd to 14th form patt.

55

PANEL B

Worked over 20 sts.

1st row (right side): P2, K2, P4, K4, P4, K2, P2.
2nd row: K2, P2, K4, P4, K4, P2, K2.
3rd row: P2, K2, P4, C4B, P4, K2, P2.
4th row: As 2nd row.
5th row: P2, [Cr3L, P2, Cr3R] twice, P2.
6th row: K3, [P2, K2] 4 times, K1.
7th row: P3, [Cr3L, Cr3R, P2] twice, P1.
8th row: K4, [P4, K4] twice.
9th row: P4, [C4B, P4] twice.
10th row: As 8th row.
11th row: P4, [K4, P4] twice.
12th to 14th rows: Work 8th to 10th rows.
15th row: P3, [Cr3R, Cr3L, P2] twice, P1.
16th row: As 6th row.
17th row: P2, [Cr3R, P2, Cr3L] twice, P2.
18th to 20th rows: Work 2nd to 4th rows.
These 20 rows form patt.

BACK

With 4mm (No 8/US 6) needles cast on 91(91:99) sts.
1st row (right side): K3, * [P1, K1 tbl] twice, P1, K3; rep from * to end.
2nd row: P2, K1, * [K1, P1 tbl] twice, P3, K1; rep from * to end.
3rd to 6th rows: Rep 1st and 2nd rows twice.
7th row: K3, * P1, sl next 2 sts onto cable needle and leave at front of work, K1 tbl, then P1, K1 tbl sts from cable needle, P1, K3; rep from * to end.
8th row: As 2nd row.
Rep last 8 rows until Back measures 19(20:21)cm/7½(8:8¼)in from beg, ending with a wrong side row.
Change to 4½mm (No 7/US 7) needles.
K 5 rows.
Inc row: K13(6:14), [M1, K11(8:12)] to last 12(5:13) sts, M1, K to end [98(102:106) sts].
Work patt as follows:
1st row (right side): [K1, P1] 4(5:6) times, P1, * K4, work 1st row of Panel A, K4 *; work 1st row of Panel B, rep from * to *, P1, [P1, K1] 4(5:6) times.
2nd row: [P1, K1] 4(5:6) times, K1, * P4, work 2nd row of Panel A, P4 *; work 2nd row of Panel B, rep from * to *, K1, [K1, P1] 4(5:6) times.
3rd row: [P1, K1] 3(4:5) times, P3, C4F, work 3rd row of Panel A, C4F, work 3rd row of Panel B, C4B, work 3rd row of Panel A, C4B, P3, [K1, P1] 3(4:5) times.
4th row: [K1, P1] 3(4:5) times, K3, * P4, work 4th row of Panel A, P4 *; work 4th row of Panel B, rep from * to *, K3, [P1, K1] 3(4:5) times.
These 4 rows set position of Panels and form double moss st at side edges.
Cont in patt as set until Back measures 53(56:60)cm/21(22:23½)in from beg, ending with a wrong side row.
Shape Shoulders
Cast off 17(17:18) sts at beg of next 2 rows and 17(18:18) sts at beg of foll 2 rows.
Leave rem 30(32:34) sts on a holder.

FRONT

Work as given for Back until Front measures 45(48:52)cm/18(19:20½)in from beg, ending with a wrong side row.
Shape Neck
Next row: Patt 43(44:45), turn.
Work on this set of sts only. Keeping patt correct, dec 1 st at neck edge on every row until 34(35:36) sts rem. Cont straight until Front matches Back to shoulder shaping, ending at side edge.
Shape Shoulders
Cast off 17(17:18) sts at beg of next row.
Patt 1 row. Cast off rem 17(18:18) sts.

With right side facing, sl centre 12(14:16) sts onto a holder, rejoin yarn to rem sts, patt to end. Complete to match first side.

SLEEVES

With 3¼mm (No 10/US 3) needles cast on 46 sts.
1st row (right side): K2, [P2, K2] to end.
2nd row: P2, [K2, P2] to end.
Rep last 2 rows until work measures 5cm/2in from beg, ending with a 1st row.
Inc row: Rib 4, [M1, rib 2, M1, rib 1] 13 times, rib 3 [72 sts].
Change to 4½mm (No 7/US 7) needles.
Work patt as follows:
1st row (right side): Work 1st row of Panel A, K4, work 1st row of Panel B, K4, work 1st row of Panel A.
2nd row: Work 2nd row of Panel A, P4, work 2nd row of Panel B, P4, work 2nd row of Panel A.
These 2 rows set position of Panels. Cont in patt as set, **at the same time**, inc 1 st at each end of next row and every foll 5th(6th:6th) row until there are 92(94:96) sts, working inc sts into patt to match Back.

Cont straight until Sleeve measures 30(32:35)cm/12(12½:13¾)in from beg, ending with a wrong side row. Cast off.

NECKBAND

Join right shoulder seam.
With 3¼mm (No 10/US 3) needles and right side facing, pick up and K24 sts down left front neck, K centre front neck sts, pick up and K24 sts up right front neck, K centre back neck sts [90(94:98) sts]. Beg with a 2nd row, work 19 rows in rib as given for Sleeve cuff. Cast off in rib.

TO MAKE UP

Wash the pieces according to the instructions given on ball band. Join left shoulder and neckband seam. Sew on sleeves, placing centre of sleeves to shoulder seams. Join side and sleeve seams.

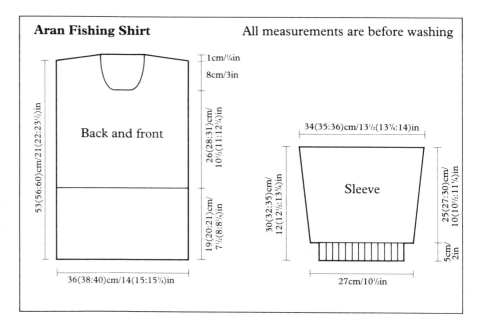

Aran Fishing Shirt
All measurements are before washing
Back and front
53(56:60)cm/21(22:23½)in
26(28:31)cm/10½(11:12½)in
1cm/¼in
8cm/3in
19(20:21)cm/7½(8¼)in
36(38:40)cm/14(15:15¼)in
34(35:36)cm/13½(13¾:14)in
Sleeve
30(32:35)cm/12(12½:13¾)in
25(27:30)cm/10(10½:11¾)in
5cm/2in
27cm/10½in

Striped Pirate Hat page 21

MATERIALS
2 25g hanks of Rowan Botany 4 ply in each of Navy (A) and White (B).
Pair each of 3mm (No 11/US 2) and 3¼mm (No 10/US 3) knitting needles.

MEASUREMENTS

To fit age	2-3 years
Length	82cm
	32¼in

TENSION
30 sts and 36 rows to 10cm/4in square over st st on 3¼mm (No 10/US 3) needles.

ABBREVIATIONS
See page 42.

TO MAKE
With 3mm (No 11/US 2) needles and A, cast on 132 sts.
Work 5cm/2in in K1, P1 rib.
Change to 3¼mm (No 10/US 3) needles.
K 1 row. P 1 row. Cont in st st and stripe patt of 12 rows B and 12 rows A throughout until work measures 16cm/6¼in from beg, ending with a P row.
Dec row: [K31, K2 tog, K2 tog tbl, K31] twice.
Patt 5 rows straight.
Dec row: [K30, K2 tog, K2 tog tbl, K30] twice.
Patt 5 rows straight.
Dec row: [K29, K2 tog, K2 tog tbl, K29] twice.
Cont in this way, dec 4 sts as set on every foll 6th row until 56 sts rem.
Cont straight until work measures approximately 84cm/33in from beg, ending with 12th row of stripe. Break off yarn, thread end through rem sts, pull up and secure. Join seam. Tie pointed end into a knot.

56

Diamonds and Bobbles Sweater

MATERIALS
13 50g balls of Rowan DK Handknit Cotton.
Pair each of 3¼mm (No 10/US 3) and 4mm (No 8/US 6) knitting needles.
Cable needle.

MEASUREMENTS

To fit age	2–4 years
Actual chest measurement	87 cm 34 in
Length	46 cm 18 in
Sleeve seam	26 cm 10¼in

TENSION
28 sts and 28 rows to 10cm/4in square over pattern on 4mm (No 8/US 6) needles.

ABBREVIATIONS
Cr4L = sl next 2 sts onto cable needle and leave at front of work, P2, then K2 from cable needle;
Cr4R = sl next 2 sts onto cable needle and leave at back of work, K2, then P2 from cable needle;
MB = make bobble as follows: [K1, P1] 3 times in next st, then pass 2nd, 3rd, 4th, 5th and 6th sts over first st;
Tw4L = sl next 2 sts onto cable needle and leave at front of work, K1, P1, then K2 from cable needle;
Tw4R = sl next 2 sts onto cable needle and leave at back of work, K2, then P1, K1 sts from cable needle.
Also see page 42.

BACK
With 3¼mm (No 10/US 3) needles cast on 122 sts.
1st row (right side): K2, [P2, K2] to end.
2nd row: P2, [K2, P2] to end.
Rep last 2 rows until welt measures 4cm/1½in from beg, ending with a 2nd row.
Change to 4mm (No 8/US 6) needles.

Work patt as follows:
1st row (right side): P1, * [K1, P1] 5 times, K4, [P1, K1] 5 times; rep from * to last st, P1.
2nd row: K1, * [P1, K1] 5 times, P4, [K1, P1] 5 times; rep from * to last st, K1.
3rd row: P1, * [K1, P1] 4 times, Cr4R, Cr4L, [P1, K1] 4 times; rep from * to last st, P1.
4th row: K1, * [P1, K1] 4 times, P2, K4, P2, [K1, P1] 4 times; rep from * to last st, K1.
5th row: P1, * [K1, P1] 3 times, Cr4R, P4, Cr4L, [P1, K1] 3 times; rep from * to last st, P1.
6th row: K1, * [P1, K1] 3 times, P2, K8, P2, [K1, P1] 3 times; rep from * to last st, K1.
7th row: P1, * [K1, P1] twice, Cr4R, P8, Cr4L, [P1, K1] twice; rep from * to last st, P1.
8th row: K1, * [P1, K1] twice, P2, K12, P2, [K1, P1] twice; rep from * to last st, K1.
9th row: P1, * K1, P1, Cr4R, P4, MB, P2, MB, P4, Cr4L, P1, K1; rep from * to last st, P1.
10th row: K1, * P1, K1, P2, K16, P2, K1, P1; rep from * to last st, K1.
11th row: P1, * Cr4R, P3, MB, P8, MB, P3, Cr4L; rep from * to last st, P1.
12th row: K1, * P2, K20, P2; rep from * to last st, K1.
13th row: P1, * K2, [P2, MB, P5, MB] twice, P2, K2; rep from * to last st, P1.
14th row: As 12th row.
15th row: P1, * Tw4L, P3, MB, P8, MB, P3, Tw4R; rep from * to last st, P1.
16th row: As 10th row.
17th row: P1, * K1, P1, Tw4L, P4, MB, P2, MB, P4, Tw4R, P1, K1; rep from * to last st, P1.
18th row: As 8th row.
19th row: P1, * [K1, P1] twice, Tw4L, P8, Tw4R, [P1, K1] twice; rep from * to last st, P1.
20th row: As 6th row.
21st row: P1, * [K1, P1] 3 times, Tw4L, P4, Tw4R, [P1, K1] 3 times; rep from * to last st, P1.
22nd row: As 4th row.
23rd row: P1, * [K1, P1] 4 times, Tw4L, Tw4R, [P1, K1] 4 times; rep from * to last st, P1.
24th row: As 2nd row.

These 24 rows form patt. Cont in patt until Back measures 46cm/18in from beg, ending with a wrong side row.
Shape Shoulders
Cast off 40 sts at beg of next 2 rows. Leave rem 42 sts on a holder.

FRONT
Work as given for Back until Front measures 38cm/15in from beg, ending with a wrong side row.
Shape Neck
Next row: Patt 52, turn.
Work on this set of sts only. Keeping patt correct, dec 1 st at neck edge on next 8 rows and 4 foll alt rows [40 sts].
Cont straight until Front matches Back to shoulder shaping, ending at side edge. Cast off.
With right side facing, sl centre 18 sts onto a holder, rejoin yarn to rem sts and patt to end. Complete to match first side of neck.

SLEEVES
With 3¼mm (No 10/US 3) needles cast on 50 sts.
Work 4cm/1½in in rib as given for Back welt, ending with a 1st row.
Inc row: Rib 2, [M1, rib 1, M1, rib 4, M1, rib 1, M1, rib 2] to end [74 sts].
Change to 4mm (No 8/US 6) needles.
Work in patt as given for Back, inc 1 st at each end of 3rd row and every foll 4th row until there are 98 sts, working inc sts into K1, P1 rib.
Cont straight until Sleeve measures 26cm/10¼in from beg, ending with a wrong side row. Cast off.

NECKBAND
Join right shoulder seam.
With 3¼mm (No 10/US 3) needles and right side facing, pick up and K24 sts down left front neck, K centre front sts, pick up and K22 sts up right front neck, K back neck sts [106 sts]. Beg with a 2nd row, work 11 rows in rib as given for Back welt. Cast off in rib.

TO MAKE UP
Join left shoulder and neckband seam. Sew on sleeves, placing centre of sleeves to shoulder seams. Join side and sleeve seams.

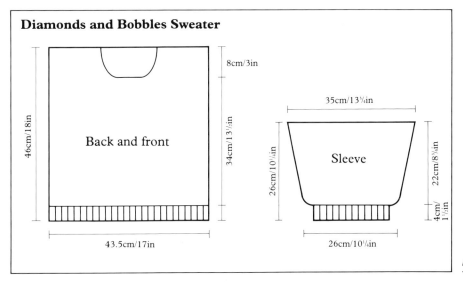

Diamonds and Bobbles Sweater

Back and front — 46cm/18in, 43.5cm/17in, 34cm/13½in, 8cm/3in

Sleeve — 35cm/13¼in, 26cm/10¼in, 22cm/8¾in, 4cm/1½in, 26cm/10¼in

Black Aran Jacket with Beanie Hat page 22

MATERIALS

Jacket: 6(7) 50g balls of Rowan
Designer DK Wool.
Pair each of 3¼mm (No 10/US 3) and
4mm (No 8/US 6) knitting needles.
One 3¼mm (No 10/US 3) circular
needle.
Cable needle.
Medium size crochet hook.
7 buttons.
Hat: 1 50g ball of Rowan Designer DK
Wool.
Pair of 4mm (No 8/US 6) knitting
needles.

MEASUREMENTS

To fit age	1–2	2–3 years
Actual chest measurement	71 28	76 cm 30 in
Length	31 12¼	34 cm 13½in
Sleeve seam	24 9½	27 cm 10¾in

TENSION

24 sts and 32 rows to 10cm/4in square
over st st on 4mm (No 8/US 6) needles.

ABBREVIATIONS

C3B = sl next st onto cable needle and
leave at back of work, K2, then K st
from cable needle;
C3F = sl next 2 sts onto cable needle
and leave at front of work, K1, then K2
from cable needle;
C4B = sl next 2 sts onto cable needle
and leave at back of work, K2, then K2
from cable needle;
C4F = sl next 2 sts onto cable needle
and leave at front of work, K2, then K2
from cable needle;
Cr3L = sl next 2 sts onto cable needle
and leave at front of work, P1, then K2
from cable needle;
Cr3R = sl next st onto cable needle and
leave at back of work, K2, then P st from
cable needle.
Also see page 42.

JACKET

PANEL A
Worked over 6 sts.
1st row (right side): P1, K4, P1.
2nd row: K1, P4, K1.
3rd row: P1, C4F, P1.
4th row: As 2nd row.
These 4 rows form patt.

PANEL B
Worked over 12 sts.
1st row (right side): P2, K8, P2.
2nd row: K2, P8, K2.
3rd row: P3, C3B, Cr3L, P3.
4th row: K3, P3, K1, P2, K3.
5th row: P2, Cr3R, K1, P1, C3F, P2.
6th row: K2, P2, K1, P1, K1, P3, K2.
7th row: P1, C3B, [P1, K1] twice, Cr3L, P1.
8th row: K1, P3, K1, [P1, K1] twice, P2, K1.
9th row: Cr3R, [K1, P1] 3 times, C3F.
10th row: P2, [K1, P1] 3 times, K1, P3.
11th row: Cr3L, [K1, P1] 3 times, Cr3R.
12th row: As 8th row.
13th row: P1, Cr3L, [P1, K1] twice, Cr3R, P1.
14th row: As 6th row.
15th row: P2, Cr3L, K1, P1, Cr3R, P2.

16th row: As 4th row.
17th row: P3, Cr3L, Cr3R, P3.
18th row: K4, P4, K4.
19th row: P2, C4B, C4F, P2.
20th row: K2, P8, K2.
21st and 22nd rows: As 1st and 2nd rows.
23rd and 24th rows: As 19th and 20th
rows.
These 24 rows form patt.

BACK
With 3¼mm (No 10/US 3) needles cast on
87(93) sts.
1st row (right side): K1, [P1, K1] to end.
2nd row: P1, [K1, P1] to end.
Rep these 2 rows until Back measures
4(5)cm/1½ (2)in from beg, ending with a
right side row.
Inc row: Rib 7, M1, [rib 6(8), M1] to last
8(6) sts, rib 8(6) [100(104) sts].
Change to 4mm (No 8/US 6) needles.
Work patt as follows:
1st row: K1, [P1, K1] 5(6) times, work 1st
row of Panel A, [work 1st row of Panel B,
then Panel A] 4 times, K1, [P1, K1] 5(6)
times.
This row sets position of Panels and forms
moss st patt at side edges.
Cont in patt as set until Back measures
31(34)cm/12¼(13½)in from beg, ending
with a wrong side row.
Shape Shoulders
Cast off 18(19) sts at beg of next 2 rows
and 18 sts at beg of foll 2 rows. Leave rem
28(30) sts on a holder.

LEFT FRONT
With 3¼mm (No 10/US 3) needles cast on
43(45) sts.
Work 4(5)cm/1½(2)in in rib as given for
Back welt, ending with a right side row.
Inc row: Rib 4(5), M1, [rib 9, M1] to last
3(4) sts, rib 3(4) [48(50) sts].
Change to 4mm (No 8/US 6) needles.
Work patt as follows:
1st row: K1, [P1, K1] 5(6) times, [work
1st row of Panel A, then Panel B] twice,
P1.
2nd row: K1, [work 2nd row of Panel B,
then Panel A] twice, K1, [P1, K1] 5(6)
times.
These 2 rows set position of Panels and
form moss st patt at side edge. Cont in patt
as set until Front measures 21(24)cm/8¼
(9½)in from beg, ending with a wrong side
row.
Shape Neck
Keeping patt correct, dec 1 st at neck edge
on next row and every foll alt row until
36(37) sts rem. Cont straight until Front
matches Back to shoulder shaping, ending
at side edge.
Shape Shoulder
Cast off 18(19) sts at beg of next row.
Work 1 row. Cast off rem 18 sts.

RIGHT FRONT
Work as given for Left Front, working patt
as follows:
1st row: P1, [work 1st row of Panel B,
then Panel A] twice, K1, [P1, K1] 5(6)
times.
2nd row: K1, [P1, K1] 5(6) times, [work
2nd row of Panel A, then Panel B] twice,
K1.
These 2 rows set position of Panels and
form moss st patt at side edge.

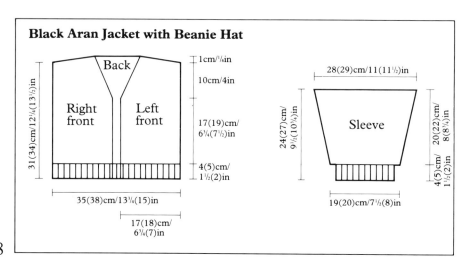

Black Aran Jacket with Beanie Hat

58

SLEEVES

With 3¼mm (No 10/US 3) needles cast on 43(45) sts.
Work 4(5)cm/1½ (2)in in rib as given for Back welt, ending with a right side row.
Inc row: Rib 4(2), M1, [rib 3, M1] to last 3(1) sts, rib 3(1) [56(60) sts].
Change to 4mm (No 8/US 6) needles.
Work patt as follows:
1st row: K1, [P1, K1] 3(4) times, work 1st row of Panel A, [work 1st row of Panel B, then Panel A] twice, K1, [P1, K1] 3(4) times.
This row sets position of Panels and forms moss st patt at side edges. Cont in patt as set, inc 1 st at each end of 2nd row and every foll 5th(6th) row until there are 78(82) sts, working inc sts into moss st patt. Cont straight until Sleeve measures 24(27)cm/9½(10¾)in from beg, ending with a wrong side row. Cast off.

FRONT BANDS AND COLLAR

Join shoulder seams.
With 3¼mm (No 10/US 3) circular needle and right side facing, pick up and K60(68) sts up straight edge of Right Front, 38 sts up shaped edge to shoulder, work across back neck sts as follows: K2(3), M1, [K3, M1] 8 times, K2(3), pick up and K38 sts down shaped edge of Left Front to beg of neck shaping and 60(68) sts down straight edge [233(251) sts].
Work backwards and forwards. Beg with a 2nd row, work 3 rows in rib as given for Back welt.
1st buttonhole row: Rib 3(4), [cast off 2, rib 10(12) sts more] 5 times, rib to end.
2nd buttonhole row: Rib to end, casting on 2 sts over those cast off in previous row.
Shape Collar
Next 2 rows: Rib to last 60(68) sts, turn, sl 1, rib to last 60(68) sts, turn.
Next 2 rows: Sl 1, rib to last 62(70) sts, turn.
Next 2 rows: Sl 1, rib to last 64(72) sts, turn.
Cont in this way, working 2 sts less at end of next 12(14) rows.
Next row: Sl 1, rib to end.
Rib 2 rows across all sts. Cast off in rib.

FLAPS (make 2)

With 4mm (No 8/US 6) needles cast on 17 sts.
1st row: K1, [P1, K1] to end.
This row forms moss st patt. Cont in patt for a further 9 rows. Dec 1 st at each end of next row and 2 foll alt rows, then at each end of foll 2 rows. Cast off.
With crochet hook, work 1 row of double crochet around row ends and cast off edge of flap. Do not turn. Now work 1 row of backward double crochet (double crochet worked from left to right). Fasten off.

TO MAKE UP

Sew on sleeves, placing centre of sleeves to shoulder seams. Join side and sleeve seams. Sew on flaps as shown in photograph and secure point with button. Sew on rem buttons to left front band.

TO MAKE

With 4mm (No 8/US 6) needles cast on 98(106) sts.
1st row: K2, [P2, K2] to end.
2nd row: P2, [K2, P2] to end.
Rep last 2 rows until work measures 15(19)cm/6(7½)in from beg, ending with a 2nd row.
Shape Top
1st row: K2, [P2 tog, K2] to end.
2nd row: P2, [K1, P2] to end.
3rd row: K2, [P1, K2] to end.
4th row: As 2nd row.
5th row: K2 tog, [P1, K2 tog] to end.
6th row: P1, [K1, P1] to end.
7th row: K1, [P3 tog, K1] to end [25(27) sts].
8th row: P1, [P2 tog] to end.
Break off yarn, thread end through rem sts, pull up and secure. Join seam, reversing seam on last 4cm/1½in for brim. Turn back brim.

Jacket with Sailor Collar and Pockets page 23

MATERIALS

8 50g balls of Rowan Designer DK Wool.
Pair each of 3¼mm (No 10/US 3) and 4mm (No 8/US 6) knitting needles.
Medium size crochet hook.
8 buttons.

MEASUREMENTS

To fit age	2–4 years
Actual chest measurement	81 cm 32 in
Length	36 cm 14 in
Sleeve seam	30 cm 11¾in

TENSION

24 sts and 32 rows to 10cm/4in square over st st on 4mm (No 8/US 6) needles.

ABBREVIATIONS

See page 42.

BACK

With 3¼mm (No 10/US 3) needles cast on 87 sts.
1st row: K1, [P1, K1] to end.
This row forms moss st patt. Cont in moss st patt until Back measures 4cm/1½in from beg and inc 2 sts evenly across last row [89 sts].
Change to 4mm (No 8/US 6) needles.
Beg with a K row, work in st st and inc 1 st at each end of 5th row and 4 foll 4th rows [99 sts]. Cont straight until Back measures 18cm/7in from beg, ending with a P row.
Shape Armholes
Cast off 5 sts at beg of next 2 rows [89 sts].
Cont straight until Back measures 25cm/10in from beg, ending with a P row.

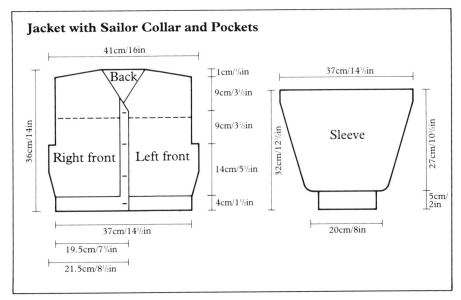

Jacket with Sailor Collar and Pockets

Back — 41cm/16in — 36cm/14in — Right front — Left front — 37cm/14½in — 19.5cm/7¼in — 21.5cm/8½in

1cm/¼in — 9cm/3½in — 9cm/3½in — 14cm/5½in — 4cm/1½in

Sleeve — 37cm/14½in — 32cm/12½in — 27cm/10½in — 5cm/2in — 20cm/8in

Now work in moss st as given for welt until Back measures 36cm/14in from beg, ending with a wrong side row.
Shape Shoulders
Cast off 13 sts at beg of next 2 rows and 12 sts at beg of foll 2 rows. Cast off rem 39 sts.

LEFT FRONT
With 3¼mm (No 10/US 3) needles cast on 45 sts.
Work 4cm/1½in in moss st patt as given for Back welt, inc 2 sts evenly across last row [47 sts].
Change to 4mm (No 8/US 6 needles).
Next row (right side): K40, moss st 7.
Next row: Moss st 7, P40.
These 2 rows form patt. Cont in patt, inc 1 st at side edge on 3rd row and 4 foll 4th rows [52 sts].
Cont straight until Front measures 18cm/7in from beg, ending at side edge.
Shape Armhole
Cast off 5 sts at beg of next row [47 sts].
Cont straight until Front measures 25cm/10in from beg, ending with a wrong side row.
Now work in moss st across all sts until Front measures 27cm/10½in from beg, ending with a wrong side row.
Shape Neck
Keeping patt correct, dec 1 st at neck edge on every row until 34 sts rem, then on every foll alt row until 25 sts rem. Cont straight for a few rows until Front matches Back to shoulder shaping, ending at armhole edge.
Shape Shoulder
Cast off 13 sts at beg of next row. Work 1 row. Cast off rem 12 sts.
Mark front edge to indicate position for 4 buttons: first one 1cm/¼in up from cast on edge, last one 1cm/¼in down from beg of neck shaping and rem 2 evenly spaced between.

RIGHT FRONT
With 3¼mm (No 10/US 3) needles cast on 45 sts.
Work 4 rows in moss st patt as given for Back welt.
1st buttonhole row (right side): Patt 2, cast off 3, patt to end.
2nd buttonhole row: Patt to last 2 sts, cast on 3 sts, patt 2.
Cont in moss st until Front measures 4cm/1½in from beg, ending with a wrong side row and inc 2 sts evenly across last row [47 sts].
Change to 4mm (No 8/US 6) needles.
Next row: Moss st 7, K40.
Next row: P40, moss st 7.
These 2 rows form patt. Complete to match Left Front, working buttonholes at markers as before.

SLEEVES
With 3¼mm (No 10/US 3) needles cast on 39 sts.
Work 5cm/2in in moss st patt as given for Back welt.
Inc row: Moss st 3, [inc in next st, moss st 3] 9 times [48 sts].
Change to 4mm (No 8/US 6) needles.
Beg with a K row, work in st st and inc 1 st at each end of every foll 3rd row until there are 88 sts. Cont straight until Sleeve measures 30cm/11¾in from beg. Mark each end of last row. Cont for a further 2cm/¾in, ending with a P row. Cast off.

COLLAR
With 4mm (No 8/US 6) needles cast on 71 sts.

Work 2cm/¾in in moss st patt as given for Back welt.
Next row (right side): Moss st 5, K61, moss st 5.
Next row: Moss st 5, P61, moss st 5.
These 2 rows form patt. Cont in patt until Collar measures 14cm/5½in from beg, ending with a wrong side row.
Shape Neck
Next row: Patt 17, cast off next 37 sts, patt to end.
Work on last set of sts only for left front collar. Patt 9 rows straight.
Dec 1 st at inside edge on next row and every foll alt row until 2 sts rem. Work 2 tog and fasten off.
With wrong side facing, rejoin yarn to rem sts for right front collar and complete to match left front collar.

POCKETS (make 2)
With 4mm (No 8/US 6) needles cast on 23 sts. Work 9cm/3½in in moss st patt as given for Back welt. Cast off.

POCKET FLAPS (make 2)
With 4mm (No 8/US 6) needles cast on 23 sts. Work 4cm/1½in in moss st patt as given for Back welt. Cont in moss st patt, dec 1 st at each end of next 6 rows.
1st buttonhole row: Work 2 tog, moss st 2, cast off 3, moss st to last 2 sts, work 2 tog.
2nd buttonhole row: Work 2 tog, moss st 1, cast on 3 sts, moss st 1, work 2 tog.

Cont in moss st, dec 1 st at each end of next 2 rows.
Next row: Sl 1, K2 tog, psso and fasten off.

STRAPS (make 2)
With 4mm (No 8/US 6) needles cast on 7 sts.
Work 8cm/3in in moss st patt as given for Back welt.
1st buttonhole row: Moss st 2, cast off 3, moss st to end.
2nd buttonhole row: Moss st 2, cast on 3, moss st to end.
Cont in moss st, work 1 row. Dec 1 st at each end of next 2 rows.
Next row: Sl 1, K2 tog, psso and fasten off.

TO MAKE UP
With crochet hook, work a row of double crochet around outer edges of collar, along cast on and side edges of pockets, along side and shaped edges of flaps and straps and along front edges of fronts. Sew on pockets and pocket flaps as shown in the photograph. Join shoulder seams. Sew on sleeves, placing centre of sleeves to shoulder seams and sewing rows above markers of sleeve tops to cast off sts at armholes. Join side and sleeve seams. Place straps on top of front welts and sew cast on edges to side seams. Sew on collar. Sew 4 buttons to right front band, one to each pocket and one on each front welt.

Boxy Jacket with Collar page 24

MATERIALS
8(9:10) 50g balls of Rowan Designer DK Wool.
Pair each of 3¼mm (No 10/US 3), 3¾mm (No 9/US 5) and 4mm (No 8/US 6) knitting needles.
Cable needle.
Medium size crochet hook.
4(5:5) buttons.

MEASUREMENTS

To fit age	3–4	4–5	5–6 years
Actual chest measurement	80 31½	84 33	88 cm 34½in
Length	36 14	39 15¼	42 cm 16½in
Sleeve seam	25 10	28 11	31 cm 12½in

TENSION
24 sts and 32 rows to 10cm/4in square over st st on 4mm (No 8/US 6) needles.

ABBREVIATIONS
C4B = sl next 2 sts onto cable needle and leave at back of work, K2, then K2 from cable needle;
C4F = sl next 2 sts onto cable needle and leave at front of work, K2, then K2 from cable needle;
Cr2L = sl next st onto cable needle and leave at front of work, P1, then K st from cable needle;

Cr2R = sl next st onto cable needle and leave at back of work, K1, then P st from cable needle;
Cr3L = sl next 2 sts onto cable needle and leave at front of work, P1, then K2 from cable needle;
Cr3R = sl next st onto cable needle and leave at back of work, K2, then P st from cable needle;
MB = make bobble as follows: [K1, P1] twice in next st, turn, K4, turn, P4, turn, K4, turn, sl 2, K2 tog, pass 2 slipped sts over.
Also see page 42.

PANEL A
Worked over 10 sts.
1st row (right side): P3, C4B, P3.
2nd row: K3, P4, K3.
3rd row: P2, Cr3R, Cr3L, P2.
4th row: K2, [P2, K2] twice.
5th row: P1, Cr3R, P2, Cr3L, P1.
6th row: K1, P2, K4, P2, K1.
7th row: P1, K2, P4, K2, P1.
8th row: As 6th row.
9th row: P1, Cr3L, P2, Cr3R, P1.
10th row: As 4th row.
11th row: P2, Cr3L, Cr3R, P2.
12th row: As 2nd row.
These 12 rows form patt.

PANEL B
Worked over 17 sts.
1st row (right side): P6, K2, P1, K2, P6.
2nd row: K6, P2, K1, P2, K6.
3rd row: P6, sl next 3 sts onto cable needle and leave at back of work, K2, then P1, K2 from cable needle, P6.
4th row: As 2nd row.
5th row: P5, Cr3R, P1, Cr3L, P5.
6th row: K5, P2, K1, P1, K1, P2, K5.
7th row: P4, Cr3R, P1, K1, P1, Cr3L, P4.
8th row: K4, P2, K1, P3, K1, P2, K4.
9th row: P3, Cr3R, P1, K3, P1, Cr3L, P3.
10th row: K3, P2, K2, P3, K2, P2, K3.
11th row: P2, Cr3R, P2, K3, P2, Cr3L, P2.
12th row: K2, P2, K3, P3, K3, P2, K2.
13th row: P1, Cr3R, P2, Cr2R, K1, Cr2L, P2, Cr3L, P1.
14th row: K1, P2, K3, P1, [K1, P1] twice, K3, P2, K1.
15th row: P1, K2, P2, Cr2R, P1, K1, P1, Cr2L, P2, K2, P1.
16th row: K1, P2, [K2, P1] 3 times, K2, P2, K1.
17th row: P1, Cr3L, P1, MB, P2, K1, P2, MB, P1, Cr3R, P1.
18th row: K2, P2, K4, P1, K4, P2, K2.
19th row: P2, Cr3L, P3, K1, P3, Cr3R, P2.
20th row: K3, P2, K3, P1, K3, P2, K3.
21st row: P3, Cr3L, P2, MB, P2, Cr3R, P3.
22nd row: K4, P2, K5, P2, K4.
23rd row: P4, Cr3L, P3, Cr3R, P4.
24th row: K5, P2, K3, P2, K5.
25th row: P5, Cr3L, P1, Cr3R, P5.
26th to 28th rows: Work 2nd to 4th rows.
29th to 32nd rows: Work 1st to 4th rows.
These 32 rows form patt.

BACK
With 3¼mm (No 10/US 3) needles cast on 111(119:127) sts.
1st row (right side): P1, [K1, P1] to end.

2nd row: K1, [P1, K1] to end.
Rep last 2 rows until Back measures 3cm/1¼in from beg, ending with a right side row.
Inc row: Rib 6(3:7), inc in next st, [rib 6(7:7), inc in next st] to last 6(3:7) sts, rib to end [126(134:142) sts].
Change to 4mm (No 8/US 6) needles.
Work patt as follows:
1st row (right side): P19(23:27), [K4, work 1st row of Panel A, K4, work 1st row of Panel B] twice, K4, work 1st row of Panel A, K4, P19(23:27).
2nd row: K1, * [K1, P1, K1] all in next st, P3 tog *; rep from * to * 3(4:5) times more, K2, [P4, work 2nd row of Panel A, P4, work 2nd row of Panel B] twice, P4, work 2nd row of Panel A, P4, K2, rep from * to * 4(5:6) times, K1.
3rd row: P19(23:27), C4F, work 3rd row of Panel A, C4F, work 3rd row of Panel B, C4F, work 3rd row of Panel A, C4B, work 3rd row of Panel B, C4B, work 3rd row of Panel A, C4B, P19(23:27).
4th row: K1, * P3 tog, [K1, P1, K1] all in next st *; rep from * to * 3(4:5) times more, K2, [P4, work 4th row of Panel A, P4, work 4th row of Panel B] twice, P4, work 4th row of Panel A, P4, K2, rep from * to * 4(5:6) times, K1.
These 4 rows set position of Panels and form patt at side edges. Cont in patt as set until Back measures 36(39:42)cm/ 14(15¼:16½)in from beg, ending with a wrong side row.
Shape Shoulders
Cast off 18(20:22) sts at beg of next 2 rows and 19(20:21) sts at beg of foll 2 rows. Cast off rem 52(54:56) sts.

LEFT FRONT
With 3¼mm (No 10/US 3) needles cast on 53(57:61) sts.
Work 3cm/1¼in in rib as given for Back welt, ending with a right side row.
Inc row: Rib 5(4:6), inc in next st, [rib 6(7:7), inc in next st] to last 5(4:6) sts, rib to end [60(64:68) sts].
Change to 4mm (No 8/US 6) needles.
Work patt as follows:
1st row (right side): P19(23:27), K4, work 1st row of Panel A, K4, work 1st row of Panel B, K4, P2.
2nd row: K2, P4, work 2nd row of Panel B, P4, work 2nd row of Panel A, P4, K2, * [K1, P1, K1] all in next st, P3 tog; rep from * 3(4:5) times more, K1.
3rd row: P19(23:27), C4F, work 3rd row of Panel A, C4F, work 3rd row of Panel B, C4F, P2.
4th row: K2, P4, work 4th row of Panel B,

P4, work 4th row of Panel A, P4, K2, * P3 tog, [K1, P1, K1] all in next st; rep from * 3(4:5) times more, K1.
These 4 rows set position of Panels and form patt at side edge. Cont in patt as set until Front measures 30(33:36)cm/11¾ (13:14¼)in from beg, ending with a right side row.
Shape Neck
Keeping patt correct, cast off 7(8:9) sts at beg of next row, 5 sts at beg of foll alt row and 3 sts at beg of foll alt row. Dec 1 st at neck edge on every row until 37(40:43) sts rem. Cont straight until Front matches Back to shoulder shaping, ending with a wrong side row.
Shape Shoulder
Cast off 18(20:22) sts at beg of next row. Patt 1 row. Cast off rem 19(20:21) sts.

RIGHT FRONT
Work as given for Left Front, reversing shapings and working patt as follows:
1st row (right side): P2, K4, work 1st row of Panel B, K4, work 1st row of Panel A, K4, P19(23:27).
2nd row: K1, * [K1, P1, K1] all in next st, P3 tog; rep from * 3(4:5) times more, K2, P4, work 2nd row of Panel A, P4, work 2nd row of Panel B, P4, K2.
3rd row: P2, C4B, work 3rd row of Panel B, C4B, work 3rd row of Panel A, C4B, P19(23:27).
4th row: K1, * P3 tog, [K1, P1, K1] all in next st; rep from * 3(4:5) times more, K2, P4, work 4th row of Panel A, P4, work 4th row of Panel B, P4, K2.
These 4 rows set position of Panels and form patt at side edge.

SLEEVES
With 3¼mm (No 10/US 3) needles cast on 45(47:49) sts.
Work 5cm/2in in rib as given for Back welt, ending with a right side row.
Inc row: Rib 1(4:0), [work twice in each of next 2 sts, rib 1] to last 2(4:1) sts, work twice in next st, rib 1(3:0) [74(74:82) sts].
Change to 4mm (No 8/US 6) needles.
Work patt as follows:
1st row (right side): P7(7:11), K4, work 1st row of Panel B, K4, work 1st row of Panel A, K4, work 1st row of Panel B, K4, P7(7:11).
2nd row: K1, * [K1, P1, K1] all in next st, P3 tog *; rep from * to * 0(0:1) time more, K2, P4, work 2nd row of Panel B, P4, work 2nd row of Panel A, P4, work 2nd row of Panel B, P4, K2, rep from * to * 1(1:2) times, K1.
3rd row: P7(7:11), C4F, work 3rd row of Panel B, C4F, work 3rd row of Panel A, C4B, work 3rd row of Panel B, C4B, P7(7:11).
4th row: K1, * P3 tog, [K1, P1, K1] all in next st *; rep from * to * 0(0:1) time more, K2, P4, work 4th row of Panel B, P4, work 4th row of Panel A, P4, work 4th row of Panel B, P4, K2, rep from * to * 1(1:2) times, K1.
These 4 rows set position of Panels and form patt at side edges. Cont in patt as set, inc 1 st at each end of next row and every foll 4th row until there are 98(106:114) sts, working inc sts into side edge patt. Cont straight until Sleeve measures 25(28:31)cm/10(11:12¼)in from beg, ending with a wrong side row. Cast off.

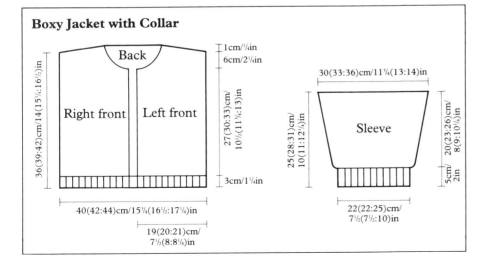

Boxy Jacket with Collar

Back

Right front | Left front

36(39:42)cm/14(15¼:16½)in

27(30:33)cm/10½(11¾:13)in

25(28:31)cm/10(11½:12¼)in

1cm/¼in

6cm/2¼in

3cm/1¼in

40(42:44)cm/15¾(16½:17¼)in

19(20:21)cm/7½(8:8¼)in

Sleeve

30(33:36)cm/11¾(13:14)in

20(23:26)cm/8(9:10¼)in

5cm/2in

22(22:25)cm/7½(7½:10)in

61

COLLAR

With 3¾mm (No 9/US 5) needles cast on 131 sts.
Beg with a 2nd row, work 3 rows in rib as given for Back welt.
Next row: Rib 5, [MB, rib 9] to last 6 sts, MB, rib 5.
Rib 1 row.
Change to 3¼mm (No 10/US 3) needles.
Cont in rib until Collar measures 6cm/2¼in from beg, ending with a wrong side row.
Dec row: Rib 9, [s1 1, K2 tog, psso, rib 7] to last 2 sts, rib 2 [107 sts].
Work a further 3 rows in rib. Cast off in rib.

BUTTONHOLE BAND

With 3¼mm (No 10/US 3) needles and right side facing, pick up and K75(81:87) sts evenly along front edge of Right Front.
Beg with a 2nd row, work 3 rows in rib as given for Back welt.
1st buttonhole row: Rib 3(3:4), [cast off 3, rib 18(14:15) sts more] 3(4:4) times, cast off 3, rib to end.
2nd buttonhole row: Rib to end, casting on 3 sts over those cast off in previous row.
Rib 4 rows. Cast off in rib.

BUTTON BAND

Work to match Buttonhole Band omitting buttonholes.

TO MAKE UP

Join shoulder seams. Sew on sleeves, placing centre of sleeves to shoulder seams. Join side and sleeve seams. With crochet hook and right side facing, work 1 row of double crochet along row ends of collar and front bands. Sew cast off edge of collar to neck edge, beginning and ending at centre of front bands. Sew on buttons.

Moss Stitch and Garter Stitch Guernsey page 25

MATERIALS

7(8) 50g balls of Rowan Designer DK Wool.
Pair of 3¼mm (No 10/US 3) and 4mm (No 8/US 6) knitting needles.

MEASUREMENTS

To fit age	3–4	5–6 years
Actual chest measurement	78 30½	88 cm 34½in
Length	42 16½	46 cm 18 in
Sleeve seam	29 11½	32 cm 12½in

TENSION

24 sts and 32 rows to 10cm/4in square over st st on 4mm (No 8/US 6) needles.

ABBREVIATIONS

See page 42.

NOTE

Read Chart from right to left on right side rows and from left to right on wrong side rows.
If other letters are required for your initials, simply chart them out on graph paper and work them in reverse stocking stitch.

BACK

With 3¼mm (No 10/US 3) needles cast on 94(106) sts.
Beg with a K row, work 6 rows in st st.
1st row (right side): K2, [P2, K2] to end.
2nd row: P2, [K2, P2] to end.
Rep last 2 rows twice more. **
Change to 4mm (No 8/US 6) needles.
*** Beg with a K row, work in st st until Back measures 21(25)cm/8¼(10)in from beg, ending with a P row.
Work yoke patt as follows:
1st and 2nd rows: K.

14

10

1

19 sts

KEY

☐ K on right side,
P on wrong side

⊡ P on right side,
K on wrong side

Moss Stitch and Garter Stitch Guernsey

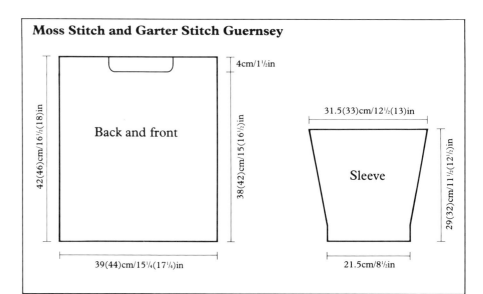

4cm/1½in

42(46)cm/16½(18)in

Back and front

38(42)cm/15(16½)in

39(44)cm/15¼(17¼)in

31.5(33)cm/12½(13)in

Sleeve

29(32)cm/11½(12½)in

21.5cm/8½in

3rd and 4th rows: P.
5th to 8th rows: Work 1st to 4th rows.
9th row: K.
10th row: P2, [K2, P2] to end.
11th row: K.
12th row: K2, [P2, K2] to end.
13th to 16th rows: Work 9th to 12th rows.
17th and 18th rows: As 9th and 10th rows.
These 18 rows form patt. Cont in patt until Back measures 30(34)cm/11¾(13½)in from beg, ending with a wrong side row.
Next row: K5, patt to last 5 sts, K5.
Rep last row until Back measures 38(42)cm/15(16½)in from beg, ending with a wrong side row. ***
Now cont in garter st (every row K) across all sts until Back measures 42(46)cm/16½(18)in from beg, ending with a wrong side row. Leave these sts on a spare needle.

FRONT
Work as given for Back to **.
Change to 4mm (No 8/US 6) needles.
Beg with a K row, work 6(8)cm/2¼(3)in in st st, ending with a P row.
Place initials as follows:
Next row: K59(67), work across 1st row of Chart, K to end.
Next row: P16(20), work across 2nd row of Chart, P to end.
Work a further 12 rows as set.
Now work as given for Back from *** to ***.
Shape Neck
Next row: K35(40), turn.
Work in garter st on this set of sts only.
Dec 1 st at neck edge on every row until 28(33) sts rem. Cont straight until Front matches Back, ending with a wrong side row. Leave these sts on a holder.
With right side facing, sl centre 24(26) sts onto a holder, rejoin yarn to rem sts, K to end. Complete to match first side.

SLEEVES
With 3¼mm (No 10/US 3) needles cast on 46 sts.
Beg with a K row, work 6 rows in st st, then work in rib as given for Back until Sleeve measures 5cm/2in from beg, ending with a wrong side row and inc 6 sts evenly across last row [52 sts].
Change to 4mm (No 8/US 6) needles.
Beg with a K row, cont in st st, inc 1 st at each end of 3rd row and every foll 5th row until there are 70 sts. Work 1 row.
Now work in yoke patt as given for Back, **at the same time,** inc 1 st at each end of 3(5) foll 4th rows, working inc sts into patt [76(80) sts].

Cont straight until Sleeve measures 29(32)cm/11½(12½)in from beg, ending with a wrong side row. Cast off.

NECKBAND
With right sides of back and front together, cast off right shoulder sts together.
With 3¼mm (No 10/US 3) needles and right side facing, pick up and K16 sts down left front neck, K centre front sts, pick up and K16 sts up right front neck, K38(40) sts from back neck, turn [94(98) sts].
K 1 row. P 2 rows. Beg with a 1st row, work 12 rows in rib as given for Back. Beg with a K row, work 4 rows in st st. Cast off.

TO MAKE UP
With right sides of back and front together, cast off left shoulder sts together. Join neckband seam, reversing seam on st st section. Sew on sleeves, placing centre of sleeves to shoulder seams. Join side and sleeve seams.

Hearts and Flowers Sweater page 28

MATERIALS
6(7) 50g balls of Rowan Nice Cotton.
Pair each of 2¾mm (No 12/US 2) and 3¼mm (No 10/US 3) knitting needles.

MEASUREMENTS

To fit age	18–24	24–36 months
Actual chest measurement	65 25½	70 cm 27½in
Length	37 14½	41 cm 16 in
Sleeve seam	23 9	27 cm 10½in

TENSION
28 sts and 36 rows to 10cm/4in square over st st on 3¼mm (No 10/US 3) needles.

ABBREVIATIONS
C2B = sl next st onto cable needle and leave at back of work, K1, then K st from cable needle;
C2F = sl next st onto cable needle and leave at front of work, K1, then K st from cable needle;
Cr2L = sl next st onto cable needle and leave at front of work, P1, then K st from cable needle;
Cr2R = sl next st onto cable needle and leave at back of work, K1, then P st from cable needle;
MB = make bobble as follows: K into front, back, front and back of next st, turn, P4, turn, K4, turn, [P2 tog] twice, turn, K2 tog;
MK = make knot as follows: [K1, P1] twice, K1 all in next st, then pass 2nd,

3rd, 4th and 5th sts over first st;
Tw2L = K into back loop of 2nd st on right hand needle, then K first st, slip both sts off needle together;
Tw2R = K into front loop of 2nd st on right hand needle, then K first st, sl both sts off needle together;
Tw2LP = K into front loop of 2nd st on right hand needle, then K first st, slip both sts off needle together;
Tw2RP = P into back loop of 2nd st on right hand needle, then K first st, slip both sts off needle together;
Tw3 = K into front loop of 3rd st on right hand needle, then K first and second sts, slip all three sts off needle together.
Also see page 42.

CANDLE TREE MOTIF
Worked over 39 sts.
1st row (right side): P39.
2nd row: K39.
3rd and 4th rows: As 1st and 2nd rows.
5th row: P18, K3, P18.
6th row: K18, P3, K18.
7th to 12th rows: Rep 5th and 6th rows 3 times.
13th row: P17, C2B, K1, C2F, P17.
14th row: K16, Cr2L, P3, Cr2R, K16.
15th row: P15, Cr2R, P1, K3, P1, Cr2L, P15.
16th row: K14, Cr2L, K2, P3, K2, Cr2R, K14.
17th row: P13, C2B, P3, K3, P3, C2F, P13.
18th row: K12, Cr2L, P1, K3, P3, K3, P1, Cr2R, K12.
19th row: P11, Cr2R, P1, K1, P3, K3, P3, K1, P1, Cr2L, P11.
20th row: K10, Cr2L, K2, P1, K3, P3, K3, P1, K2, Cr2R, K10.
21st row: P9, C2B, P3, yon, K1, yrn, P3,

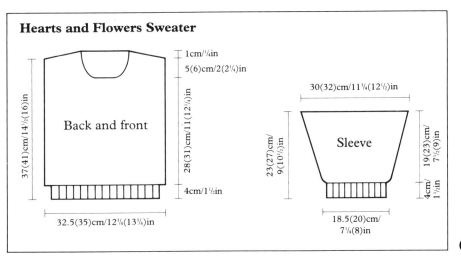

Hearts and Flowers Sweater

Back and front
37(41)cm/14½(16)in
28(31)cm/11(12½)in
1cm/¼in
5(6)cm/2(2¼)in
4cm/1½in
32.5(35)cm/12¾(13¾)in

Sleeve
30(32)cm/11¾(12½)in
23(27)cm/9(10½)in
19(23)cm/7½(9)in
4cm/1½in
18.5(20)cm/7¼(8)in

K3, P3, yon, K1, yrn, P3, C2F, P9.
22nd row: K8, Cr2L, P1, [K3, P3] 3 times, K3, P1, Cr2R, K8.
23rd row: P7, Cr2R, P1, K1, P3, [K1, yf] twice, K1, P3, K3, P3, [K1, yf] twice, K1, P3, K1, P1, Cr2L, P7.
24th row: K6, Cr2L, K2, P1, K3, P5, K3, P3, K3, P5, K3, P1, K2, Cr2R, K6.
25th row: P5, Cr2R, P3, K1, P3, K2, yf, K1, yf, K2, P3, K3, P3, K2, yf, K1, yf, K2, P3, K1, P3, Cr2L, P5.
26th row: K5, P1, K4, P1, K3, P7, K3, P3, K3, P7, K3, P1, K4, P1, K5.
27th row: P5, yon, K1, yrn, P4, K1, P3, skpo, K3, K2 tog, P3, K3, P3, skpo, K3, K2 tog, P3, K1, P4, yon, K1, yrn, P5.
28th row: K5, P3, K4, P1, K3, P5, K3, P3, K3, P5, K3, P1, K4, P3, K5.
29th row: P5, [K1, yf] twice, K1, P4, K1, P3, skpo, K1, K2 tog, P3, K3, P3, skpo, K1, K2 tog, P3, K1, P4, [K1, yf] twice, K1, P5.
30th row: K5, P5, K4, P1, [K3, P3] 3 times, K3, P1, K4, P5, K5.
31st row: P5, K2, yf, K1, yf, K2, P4, yon, K1, yrn, P3, sl 1, K2 tog, psso, P2, Cr2R, K1, Cr2L, P2, sl 1, K2 tog, psso, P3, yon, K1, yrn, P4, K2, yf, K1, yf, K2, P5.
32nd row: K5, P7, K4, P3, K6, [P1, K1] twice, P1, K6, P3, K4, P7, K5.
33rd row: P5, skpo, K3, K2 tog, P4, [K1, yf] twice, K1, P5, Cr2R, P1, K1, P1, Cr2L, P5, [K1, yf] twice, K1, P4, skpo, K3, K2 tog, P5.
34th row: K5, P5, K4, P5, K5, [P1, K2] twice, P1, K5, P5, K4, P5, K5.
35th row: P5, skpo, K1, K2 tog, P4, K2, yf, K1, yf, K2, P4, Cr2R, P2, K1, P2, Cr2L, P4, K2, yf, K1, yf, K2, P4, skpo, K1, K2 tog, P5.
36th row: K5, P3, K4, P7, K4, [P1, K3] twice, P1, K4, P7, K4, P3, K5.
37th row: P5, sl 1, K2 tog, psso, P4, skpo, K3, K2 tog, P3, Cr2R, P3, K1, P3, Cr2L, P3, skpo, K3, K2 tog, P4, sl 1, K2 tog, psso, P5.
38th row: K10, P5, K3, [P1, K4] twice, P1, K3, P5, K10.
39th row: P10, skpo, K1, K2 tog, P3, yon, K1, yrn, P4, K1, P4, yon, K1, yrn, P3, skpo, K1, K2 tog, P10.
40th row: K10, P3, K3, P3, K4, P1, K4, P3, K3, P3, K10.
41st row: P10, sl 1, K2 tog, psso, P3, [K1, yf] twice, [K1, P4] twice, [K1, yf] twice, K1, P3, sl 1, K2 tog, psso, P10.
42nd row: K14, P5, K4, P1, K4, P5, K14.
43rd row: P14, K2, yf, K1, yf, K2, P4, yon, K1, yrn, P4, K2, yf, K1, yf, K2, P14.
44th row: K14, P7, K4, P3, K4, P7, K14.
45th row: P14, skpo, K3, K2 tog, P4, [K1, yf] twice, K1, P4, skpo, K3, K2 tog, P14.
46th row: K14, [P5, K4] twice, P5, K14.
47th row: P14, skpo, K1, K2 tog, P4, K2, yf, K1, yf, K2, P4, skpo, K1, K2 tog, P14.
48th row: K14, P3, K4, P7, K4, P3, K14.
49th row: P14, sl 1, K2 tog, psso, P4, skpo, K3, K2 tog, P4, sl 1, K2 tog, psso, P14.
50th row: K19, P5, K19.
51st row: P19, skpo, K1, K2 tog, P19.
52nd row: K19, P3, K19.
53rd row: P19, sl 1, K2 tog, psso, P19.
54th row: K39.
55th to 58th rows: Work 1st to 4th rows.

FLOWER GARDEN MOTIF
Worked over 37 sts.
1st row (right side): P37.
2nd row: K37.
3rd row: P12, [K1 tbl, P11] twice, P1.
4th row: K12, [P1 tbl, K11] twice, K1.
5th to 8th rows: Rep 3rd and 4th rows twice.

9th row: P8, [yb, insert right hand needle from front before K tbl st on 3rd row, catch yarn at back and draw through long loop, K next st, then pass loop over the K st, P3, K1 tbl, P3, yb, insert right hand needle from front after K tbl st on 3rd row, catch yarn at back and draw through long loop, K next st, then pass loop over the K st, P3] twice, P5.
10th row: As 4th row.
11th row: P12, *[K1, yf] 3 times, K1 all in next st, P11; rep from * once more, P1.
12th row: K12, [P7, K11] twice, K1.
13th row: P12, [skpo, sl 1, K2 tog, psso, K2 tog, P11] twice, P1.
14th row: K12, [P3 tog, K11] twice, K1.
15th row: [P6, K1 tbl, P5] 3 times, P1.
16th row: [K6, P1 tbl, K5] 3 times, K1.
17th to 20th rows: Rep 15th and 16th rows twice.
21st row: [P2, yb, insert right hand needle from front before K tbl st on 15th row, catch yarn at back and draw through long loop, K next st, then pass loop over the K st, P3, K1 tbl, P3, yb, insert right hand needle from front after K tbl st on 15th row, catch yarn at back and draw through long loop, K next st, then pass loop over the K st, P1] 3 times, P1.
22nd row: As 16th row.
23rd row: * P6, [K1, yf] 3 times, K1 all in next st, P5; rep from * twice more, P1.
24th row: [K6, P7, K5] 3 times, K1.
25th row: [P6, skpo, sl 1, K2 tog, psso, K2 tog, P5] 3 times, P1.
26th row: [K6, P3 tog, K5] 3 times, K1.
27th and 28th rows: As 1st and 2nd rows.

BOBBLE HEART MOTIF
Worked over 21 sts.
1st row (right side): P21.
2nd row and every foll alt row: K21.
3rd row: P21.
5th row: P10, MB, P10.
7th row: P8, MB, P3, MB, P8.
9th row: P6, MB, P7, MB, P6.
11th row: P21.
13th row: P4, MB, P11, MB, P4.
15th row: P4, [MB, P5] twice, MB, P4.
17th row: P6, MB, P1, MB, P3, MB, P1, MB, P6.
19th row: P21.
21st row: P21.
22nd row: K21.

MEDALLION WITH LEAF MOTIF
Worked over 23 sts.
1st row (right side): P23.
2nd row: K23.
3rd row: P23.
4th row: K10, P3, K10.
5th row: P10, Tw3, P10.
6th row: As 4th row.
7th row: P9, Tw2R, K1 tbl, Tw2L, P9.

8th row: K8, Tw2RP, K1, P1, K1, Tw2LP, K8.
9th row: P7, Tw2R, K2, K1 tbl, K2, Tw2L, P7.
10th row: K7, [P1, K3] twice, P1, K7.
11th row: P6, Tw2R, K3, K1 tbl, K3, Tw2L, P6.
12th row: K6, [P1, K4] twice, P1, K6.
13th row: P5, Tw2R, K2, Tw2LP, K1 tbl, Tw2RP, K2, Tw2L, P5.
14th row: K5, P1, K2, Tw2LP, K1, P1, K1, Tw2LP, K2, P1, K5.
15th row: P4, Tw2R, K1, Tw2LP, P2, K1 tbl, P2, Tw2RP, K1, Tw2L, P4.
16th row: K4, P1, K2, [P1, K3] twice, P1, K2, P1, K4.
17th row: P4, K4, P3, [K1, yf, K1, yf, K1] all in next st, P3, K4, P4.
18th row: K4, P1, K2, P1, K3, P5, K3, P1, K2, P1, K4.
19th row: P4, K4, P3, K5, P3, K4, P4.
20th row: As 18th row.
21st row: P4, K4, P3, skpo, K1, K2 tog, P3, K4, P4.
22nd row: K4, P1, K2, P1, K3, P3, K3, P1, K2, P1, K4.
23rd row: P4, K3, Tw2L, P2, sl 1, K2 tog, psso, P2, Tw2R, K3, P4.
24th row: K4, P1, K3, P1, K5, P1, K3, P1, K4.
25th row: P4, Tw2RP, K2, Tw2L, P3, Tw2R, K2, Tw2LP, P4.
26th row: K5, [P1, K3] 3 times, P1, K5.
27th row: P5, Tw2RP, K2, Tw2L, P1, Tw2R, K2, Tw2LP, P5.
28th row: K6, P1, K3, P1, K1, P1, K3, P1, K6.
29th row: P6, Tw2RP, K2, Tw3, K2, Tw2LP, P6.
30th row: K7, [P1, K7] twice.
31st row: P7, Tw2RP, K5, Tw2LP, P7.
32nd row: K8, Tw2LP, K3, Tw2RP, K8.
33rd row: P9, Tw2RP, K1, Tw2LP, P9.
34th and 35th rows: As 4th and 5th rows.
36th row: K23.
37th row: P23.

PANEL A
Worked over 7 sts.
1st row (right side): P3, MK, P3.
2nd to 4th rows: P7.
These 4 rows form patt.

FRONT
With 2¾mm (No 12/US 2) needles cast on 75(83) sts.
Work rib patt as follows:
1st row (right side): K3, [P2, MK, P2, K3] to end.
2nd row: P3, [K5, P3] to end.
3rd row: K3, [P5, K3] to end.
4th row: As 2nd row.
These 4 rows form rib patt. Work a further 11 rows in rib patt.
Inc row: Rib 3(6), [M1, rib 5, M1, rib 4(6)] to end [91(97) sts].
Change to 3¼mm (No 10/US 3) needles.
Beg with a K row, work 2(8) rows in st st.
Place Candle Tree Motif as follows:
1st row: K45(49), work 1st row of Candle Tree Motif, K7(9).
2nd row: P7(9), work 2nd row of Candle Tree Motif, P45(49).
Work a further 10 rows as set.
Place Flower Garden Motif as follows:
Next row: K3(5), work 1st row of Flower Garden Motif, K5(7), work 13th row of Candle Tree Motif, K7(9).
Next row: P7(9), work 14th row of Candle Tree Motif, P5(7), work 2nd row of Flower Garden Motif, P3(5).
Work a further 26 rows as set.
Next row: K45(49), work 41st row of Candle Tree Motif, K7(9).

Next row: P7(9), work 42nd row of Candle Tree Motif, P45(49).
Work a further 16 rows as set.
Beg with a K row, work 0(4) rows in st st.
Place Bobble Heart Motif as follows:
Next row: K15(17), work 1st row of Bobble Heart Motif, K55(59).
Next row: P55(59), work 2nd row of Bobble Heart Motif, P15(17).
Work a further 2 rows as set.
Place Medallion with Leaf Motif and Panel A as follows:
Next row: K4(5), work 1st row of Panel A, K4(5), work 5th row of Bobble Heart Motif, K11(13), work 1st row of Medallion with Leaf Motif, K10(11), work 1st row of Panel A, K4(5).
Next row: P4(5), work 2nd row of Panel A, P10(11), work 2nd row of Medallion with Leaf Motif, P11(13), work 6th row of Bobble Heart Motif, P4(5), work 2nd row of Panel A, P4(5).
Work a further 16 rows as set.
Next row: K4(5), work 3rd row of Panel A, K36(39), work 19th row of Medallion with Leaf Motif, K10(11), work 3rd row of Panel A, K4(5).
Next row: P4(5), work 4th row of Panel A, P10(11), work 20th row of Medallion with Leaf Motif, P36(39), work 4th row of Panel A, P4(5).
Work a further 17 rows as set.
Next row: P4(5), work 2nd row of Panel A, P69(73), work 2nd row of Panel A, P4(5).
Cont in st st with Panels A at side edges as set, work as follows:
Shape Neck
Next row: Patt 35(37), turn.
Work on this set of sts only. Dec 1 st at neck edge on every row until 27(29) sts rem. Cont straight until Front measures 37(41)cm/14½(16)in from beg, ending at side edge.
Shape Shoulders
Cast off 13(15) sts at beg of next row.
Work 1 row. Cast off rem 14 sts. With right side facing, sl centre 21(23) sts onto a holder, rejoin yarn to rem sts and patt to end. Complete to match first side.

BACK
Work as given for Front to shoulder shaping, ending with a wrong side row but omitting neck shaping.
Shape Shoulders
Cast off 13(15) sts at beg of next 2 rows and 14 sts at beg of foll 2 rows. Leave rem 37(39) sts on a holder.

SLEEVES
With 2¾mm (No 12/US 2) needles cast on 43 sts.
Work 15 rows in rib patt as given for Front welt.
Inc row: Rib 3(4), M1, [rib 5(3), M1, rib 4, M1] to last 4 sts, rib 4 [52(54) sts].
Change to 3¼mm (No 10/US 3) needles.
Beg with a K row, work 2(6) rows in st st inc 1 st at each end of 4th row on 2nd size only [52(56) sts].

Place Flower Garden Motif as follows:
Next row: K twice in first st, K9(11), work 1st row of Flower Garden Motif, K4(6), K twice in last st.
Next row: P6(8), work 2nd row of Flower Garden Motif, P11(13).
Work a further 26 rows as set, **at the same time**, inc 1 st at each end of 2nd row and every foll 3rd row, working inc sts into st st [72(76) sts].
Beg with a K row, work 2 rows in st st.
Place Medallion with Leaf Motif as follows:
Next row: K twice in first st, K3(5), work 1st row of Medallion with Leaf Motif, K44(46), K twice in last st.
Next row: P46(48), work 2nd row of Medallion with Leaf Motif, P5(7).
Work a further 2 rows as set, inc one st at each end of last row [76(80) sts].
Place Bobble Heart Motif as follows:
Next row: K6(8), work 5th row of Medallion with Leaf Motif, K11, work 1st row of Bobble Heart Motif, K15(17).
Next row: P15(17), work 2nd row of Bobble Heart Motif, P11, work 6th row of Medallion with Leaf Motif, P6(8).
Work a further 20 rows as set, inc 1 st at each end of next row and 3(4) foll 3rd rows [84(90) sts].
Next row: K10(13), work 27th row of Medallion with Leaf Motif, K51(54).
Next row: P51(54), work 28th row of Medallion with Leaf Motif, P10(13).

Work a further 9 rows as set. Beg with a P row, work 1(9) rows in st st.
Cast off.

NECKBAND
Join right shoulder seam.
With 2¾mm (No 12/US 2) needles and right side facing, pick up and K17(19) sts down left front neck, K centre front sts, pick up and K16(18) sts up right front neck, K back neck sts [91(99) sts].
Beg with a 2nd row, work 13 rows in rib patt as given for Front welt.
Cast off in rib.

TO MAKE UP
Join left shoulder and neckband seam. Sew on sleeves, placing centre of sleeves to shoulder seams. Join side and sleeve seams.

Aran Cardigan with Lace Edging page 29

MATERIALS
7(8:9) 50g balls of Rowan Cotton Glace.
Pair each of 2¾mm (No 12/US 2) and 3¼mm (No 10/US 3) knitting needles.
4 buttons.
Cable needle.

MEASUREMENTS

To fit age	1	2	3 years
Actual chest measurement	66 26	70 27½	75 cm 29½in
Length	31 12¼	33 13	35 cm 13¾in
Sleeve seam	21 8¼	23 9	26 cm 10¼in

TENSION
28 sts and 36 rows to 10cm/4in square over double moss stitch on 3¼mm (No 10/US 3) needles.

ABBREVIATIONS
C2B = sl next st onto cable needle and leave at back of work, K1, then K st from cable needle;
C2F = sl next st onto cable needle and leave at front of work, K1, then K st from cable needle;
C4B = sl next 2 sts onto cable needle and leave at back of work, K2, then K2 from cable needle;
C4F = sl next 2 sts onto cable needle and leave at front of work, K2, then K2 from cable needle;
Cr2L = sl next st onto cable needle and leave at front of work, P1, then K st from cable needle;
Cr2R = sl next st onto cable needle and

Aran Cardigan with Lace Edging

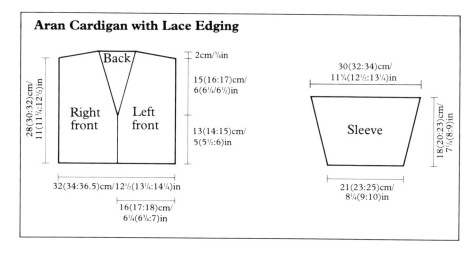

leave at back of work, K1, then P st from cable needle;

Cr3L = sl next 2 sts onto cable needle and leave at front of work, P1, then K2 from cable needle;

Cr3R = sl next st onto cable needle and leave at back of work, K2, then P st from cable needle;

MB = make bobble as follows: [K1, P1, K1, P1] all in next st, turn, P4, turn, K4, then pass 2nd, 3rd and 4th st over first st.

Also see page 42.

PANEL A
Worked over 16 sts.
1st row (right side): * P6, C2B **, C2F, P6 ***.
2nd row: * K5, Cr2L, P1 **, P1, Cr2R, K5 ***.
3rd row: * P4, Cr2R, C2B **, C2F, Cr2L, P4 ***.
4th row: * K3, Cr2L, K1, P2 **, P2, K1, Cr2R, K3 ***.
5th row: * P2, Cr2R, P1, Cr2R, K1 **, K1, Cr2L, P1, Cr2L, P2 ***.
6th row: * [K2, P1] twice, K1, P1 **, P1, K1, [P1, K2] twice ***.
7th row: * P2, MB, P1, Cr2R, P1, K1 **, K1, P1, Cr2L, P1, MB, P2 ***.
8th row: * K4, P1, K2, P1 **, P1, K2, P1, K4 ***.
9th row: * P4, MB, P2, K1 **, K1, P2, MB, P4 ***.
10th row: * K7, P1 **, P1, K7 ***.
These 10 rows form patt.

PANEL B
Worked over 9 sts.
1st row (right side): P1, Cr3L, P5.
2nd row: K5, P2, K2.
3rd row: P1, K1, Cr3L, P4.
4th row: K4, P2, K1, P1, K1.
5th row: P2, K1, Cr3L, P3.
6th row: K3, P2, K1, P1, K2.
7th row: [P1, K1] twice, Cr3L, P2.
8th row: K2, P2, [K1, P1] twice, K1.
9th row: P2, K1, P1, K1, Cr3L, P1.
10th row: K1, P2, [K1, P1] twice, K2.
11th row: P1, [K1, P1] twice, Cr3R, P1.
12th row: As 8th row.
13th row: P2, K1, P1, Cr3R, P2.
14th row: As 6th row.
15th row: P1, K1, P1, Cr3R, P3.
16th row: As 4th row.
17th row: P2, Cr3R, P4.
18th row: As 2nd row.
19th row: P1, Cr3R, P5.
20th row: K6, P2, K1.
These 20 rows form patt.

PANEL C
Worked over 9 sts.
1st row (right side): P5, Cr3R, P1.
2nd row: K2, P2, K5.
3rd row: P4, Cr3R, K1, P1.
4th row: K1, P1, K1, P2, K4.
5th row: P3, Cr3R, K1, P2.
6th row: K2, P1, K1, P2, K3.
7th row: P2, Cr3R, [K1, P1] twice.
8th row: K1, [P1, K1] twice, P2, K2.
9th row: P1, Cr3R, [K1, P1] twice, P1.
10th row: K2, [P1, K1] twice, P2, K1.
11th row: P1, Cr3L, [P1, K1] twice, P1.
12th row: As 8th row.
13th row: P2, Cr3L, P1, K1, P2.
14th row: As 6th row.
15th row: P3, Cr3L, P1, K1, P1.
16th row: As 4th row.
17th row: P4, Cr3L, P2.
18th row: As 2nd row.
19th row: P5, Cr3L, P1.
20th row: K1, P2, K6.
These 20 rows form patt.

BACK
With 3¼mm (No 10/US 3) needles cast on 110(114:122) sts.
Work patt as follows:
1st row (right side): [K1, P1] 5(6:8) times, K4, work 1st row of Panel A from * to ***, K4, work 1st row of Panel B, K4, work 1st row of Panel A from * to ***, K4, work 1st row of Panel C, K4, work 1st row of Panel A from * to ***, K4, [K1, P1] 5(6:8) times.
2nd row: [P1, K1] 5(6:8) times, P4, work 2nd row of Panel A from * to ***, P4, work 2nd row of Panel C, P4, work 2nd row of Panel A from * to ***, P4, work 2nd row of Panel B, P4, work 2nd row of Panel A from * to ***, P4, [K1, P1] 5(6:8) times.
3rd row: [P1, K1] 4(5:7) times, P2, C4F, work 3rd row of Panel A from * to ***, C4B, work 3rd row of Panel B, C4F, work 3rd row of Panel A from * to ***, C4B, work 3rd row of Panel C, C4F, work 3rd row of Panel A from * to ***, C4B, P2, [K1, P1] 4(5:7) times.
4th row: [K1, P1] 4(5:7) times, K2, P4, work 4th row of Panel A from * to ***, P4, work 4th row of Panel C, P4, work 4th row of Panel A from * to ***, P4, work 4th row of Panel B, P4, work 4th row of Panel A from * to ***, P4, K2, [P1, K1] 4(5:7) times.
These 4 rows set position of Panels and form double moss st patt at side edges.
Cont in patt as set until Back measures 28(30:32)cm/11(11¾:12½)in from beg, ending with a wrong side row.
Shape Shoulders
Cast off 12(12:13) sts at beg of next 4 rows and 11(12:13) sts at beg of foll 2 rows.
Cast off rem 40(42:44) sts.

LEFT FRONT
With 3¼mm (No 10/US 3) needles cast on 56(58:62) sts.
Work patt as follows:
1st row (right side): [K1, P1] 5(6:8) times, K4, work 1st row of Panel A from * to ***, K4, work 1st row of Panel B, K4, work 1st row of Panel A from * to **, K1.
2nd row: P1, work 2nd row of Panel A from ** to ***, P4, work 2nd row of Panel B, P4, work 2nd row of Panel A from * to ***, P4, [K1, P1] 5(6:8) times.
3rd row: [P1, K1] 4(5:7) times, P2, C4F, work 3rd row of Panel A from * to ***, C4B, work 3rd row of Panel B, C4F, work 3rd row of Panel A from * to **, K1.
4th row: P1, work 4th row of Panel A from ** to ***, P4, work 4th row of Panel B, P4, work 4th row of Panel A from * to ***, K2, [P1, K1] 4(5:7) times.
These 4 rows set position of Panels and form double moss st patt at side edge. Cont in patt as set until Front measures 13(14:15)cm/5(5½:6)in from beg, ending with a wrong side row.
Shape Neck
Keeping patt correct, dec 1 st at front edge on next row and every foll alt row until 43(45:49) sts rem, then on every foll 3rd row until 35(36:39) sts rem. Cont straight until Front matches Back to shoulder shaping, ending at side edge.
Shape Shoulder
Cast off 12(12:13) sts at beg of next row and foll alt row. Patt 1 row. Cast off rem 11(12:13) sts.

RIGHT FRONT
With 3¼mm (No 10/US 3) needles cast on 56(58:62) sts.
Work patt as follows:
1st row (right side): K1, work 1st row of Panel A from ** to ***, K4, work 1st row of Panel C, K4, work 1st row of Panel A from * to ***, K4, [P1, K1] 5(6:8) times.
2nd row: [P1, K1] 5(6:8) times, P4, work 2nd row of Panel A from * to ***, P4, work 2nd row of Panel C, P4, work 2nd row of Panel A from * to **, P1.
3rd row: K1, work 3rd row of Panel A from ** to ***, C4B, work 3rd row of Panel C, C4F, work 3rd row of Panel A from * to ***, C4B, P2, [K1, P1] 4(5:7) times.
4th row: [K1, P1] 4(5:7) times, K2, P4, work 4th row of Panel A from * to ***, P4, work 4th row of Panel C, P4, work 4th row of Panel A from * to **, P1.
These 4 rows set position of Panels and form double moss st patt at side edges.
Complete to match Left Front.

SLEEVES
With 3¼mm (No 10/US 3) needles cast on 70(74:78) sts.
Work patt as follows:
1st row (right side): [K1, P1] 5(6:7) times, K4, work 1st row of Panel B, K4, work 1st row of Panel A from * to ***, K4, work 1st row of Panel C, K4, [P1, K1] 5(6:7) times.
2nd row: [P1, K1] 5(6:7) times, P4, work 2nd row of Panel C, P4, work 2nd row of Panel A from * to ***, P4, work 2nd row of Panel B, P4, [K1, P1] 5(6:7) times.
3rd row: [P1, K1] 4(5:6) times, P2, C4B, work 3rd row of Panel B, C4F, work 3rd row of Panel A from * to ***, C4B, work 3rd row of Panel C, C4F, P2, [K1, P1] 4(5:6) times.
4th row: [K1, P1] 4(5:6) times, K2, P4, work 4th row of Panel C, P4, work 4th row of Panel A from * to ***, P4, work 4th row of Panel B, P4, K2, [P1, K1] 4(5:6) times.

These 4 rows set position of Panels and form double moss st patt at side edges. Cont in patt as set, inc 1 st at each end of next row and every foll 4th(4th:5th) row until there are 92(98:104) sts, working inc sts into double moss st patt. Cont straight until Sleeve measures 18(20:23)cm/7¼(8:9)in from beg, ending with a wrong side row. Cast off.

COLLAR

Join shoulder seams.
With 3¼mm (No 10/US 3) needles and wrong side facing, pick up and K35(38:41) sts up right front neck, 26(28:30) sts across back neck, 35(38:41) sts down left front neck [96(104:112) sts].
Beg with a K row, work in reverse st st throughout, dec 1 st at each end of 3 foll alt rows.
Next row: K32(35:38), [M1, K6(6:7)] twice, M1, K2(4:2), M1, [K6(6:7), M1] twice, K to end.
Work 3 rows, dec 1 st at each end of 1st and 3rd rows [92(100:108) sts].
Next row: K2 tog, K28(31:34), [M1, K7(7:8)] twice, M1, K4(6:4), M1, [K7(7:8), M1] twice, K to last 2 sts, K2 tog.
Work 3 rows, dec 1 st at each end of every row [90(98:106) sts].
Next row: K2 tog, K24(27:30), [M1, K8(8:9)] twice, M1, K6(8:6), M1, [K8(8:9), M1] twice, K to last 2 sts, K2 tog.
Work 3 rows, dec 1 st at each end of every row [88(96:104) sts].

Next row: K22(25:28), [M1, K9(9:10)] twice, M1, K8(10:8), M1, [K9(9:10), M1] twice, K to end.
Cast off 3 sts at beg of next 4 rows. Cast off rem 82(90:98) sts.

BUTTON BAND

With 2¾mm (No 12/US 2) needles cast on 8 sts.
Work in P1, K1 rib until band when slightly stretched, fits along front edge of Left Front to beg of neck shaping. Cast off in rib. Sew in place.
Mark band to indicate position of 4 buttons: first one 2cm/¾in up from cast on edge, last one 1cm/¼in down from cast off edge and rem 2 evenly spaced between.

BUTTONHOLE BAND

With 2¾mm (No 12/US 2) needles cast on 8 sts.
Work in K1, P1 rib until first marker on Button Band is reached.
* **1st buttonhole row (right side):** Rib 3, cast off 2, rib to end.
2nd buttonhole row: Rib 3, cast on 2 sts, rib to end.
Cont in rib until next marker is reached, ending with a wrong side row *.
Rep from * to * 2 times more, then work the 2 buttonhole rows again.
Rib 2 rows. Cast off in rib. Sew in place.

COLLAR EDGING

With 2¾mm (No 12/US 2) needles cast on 4 sts. K 1 row.
1st row (right side): K2, yf, K2.

2nd row and 2 foll alt rows: Sl, 1, K to end.
3rd row: K3, yf, K2.
5th row: K2, yf, K2 tog, yf, K2.
7th row: K3, yf, K2 tog, yf, K2.
8th row: Cast off 4, K to end.
These 8 rows form patt. Cont in patt until edging, when slightly stretched, fits around outside edge of collar, ending with 8th row of patt. Cast off.

CUFF EDGINGS

Work as given for Collar Edging, until edging, when slightly stretched, fits along lower edge of sleeve, ending with 8th row of patt. Cast off.

WELT EDGING

Work as given for Collar Edging, until edging, when slightly stretched, fits along lower edges of Fronts and Back, ending with 8th row of patt. Cast off.

TO MAKE UP

Sew on cuff edgings. Placing centre of sleeves to shoulder seams, sew on sleeves. Join side and sleeve seams. Sew on collar and welt edgings. Join cast on and off edges of collar edging to front bands. Sew on buttons.

Bobbles and Waves Sweater with Bag page 30

MATERIALS

Sweater: 11(12:13) 50g balls of Rowan Den-M-nit Indigo Cotton DK.
Pair each of 3¼mm (No 10/US 3) and 4½mm (No 7/US 7) knitting needles.
Cable needle.

Bag: 3 50g balls of Rowan Den-M-nit Indigo Cotton DK.
Pair of 4mm (No 8/US 6) knitting needles.

MEASUREMENTS

To fit age	3–4	4–5	5–6 years
The following measurements are after the garment has been washed to the instructions given on ball band.			
Actual chest measurement	98 38½	102 40	106 cm 41½in
Length	42 16½	45 17¾	48 cm 19 in
Sleeve seam	25 10	28 11	31 cm 12¼in

TENSION

20 sts and 34 rows to 10cm/4in square over double moss stitch on 4½mm (No 7/US 7) needles.

ABBREVIATIONS

C4B = sl next 2 sts onto cable needle and leave at back of work, K2, then K2 from cable needle;
C4F = sl next 2 sts onto cable needle and leave at front of work, K2, then K2 from cable needle;
Cr3L = sl next 2 sts onto cable needle and leave at front of work, P1, then K2 from cable needle;
Cr3R = sl next st onto cable needle and leave at back of work, K2, then P st from cable needle;

Cr4L = sl next 2 sts onto cable needle and leave at front of work, P2, then K2 from cable needle;
Cr4R = sl next 2 sts onto cable needle and leave at back of work, K2, then P2 from cable needle;
Cr5L = sl next 2 sts onto cable needle and leave at front of work, P3, then K2 from cable needle;
Cr5R = sl next 3 sts onto cable needle and leave at back of work, K2, then P3 from cable needle;
MB = make bobble as follows: K into front, back and front of next st, [turn, K3] 3 times, turn, sl 1, K2 tog, psso, leave bobble on right side of work;
MK = make knot as follows: [K1, P1] 3 times in next st, then pass 2nd, 3rd, 4th, 5th and 6th sts over first st;
Tw2L = K into the back loop of second st on right hand needle, then K tog first and second sts, slip both sts off needle;
Tw2R = K into the front loop of second st on right hand needle, then K first st, sl both sts off needle;
Tw4L = sl next 2 sts onto cable needle and leave at front of work, K1, P1, then K2 from cable needle;
Tw4R = sl next 2 sts onto cable needle and leave at back of work, K2, then P1, K1 from cable needle.
Also see page 42.

PANEL A
Worked over 16 sts.
1st row (right side): P2, K2, [P1, K1] 5 times, P2.
2nd row: K2, [P1, K1] 5 times, P2, K2.
3rd row: P2, Cr4L, [P1, K1] 4 times, P2.
4th row: K2, [P1, K1] 4 times, P2, K4.
5th row: P4, Cr4L, [P1, K1] 3 times, P2.
6th row: K2, [P1, K1] 3 times, P2, K6.
7th row: P6, Cr4L, [P1, K1] twice, P2.
8th row: K2, [P1, K1] twice, P2, K8.
9th row: P3, MK, P4, Cr4L, P1, K1, P2.
10th row: K2, P1, K1, P2, K10.
11th row: P6, MK, P3, Cr4L, P2.
12th row: K2, P2, K12.
13th row: P3, MK, P5, MK, P2, K2, P2.
14th row: As 12th row,
15th row: P6, MK, P3, Tw4R, P2.
16th row: As 10th row.
17th row: P3, MK, P4, Tw4R, P1, K1, P2.
18th row: As 8th row.
19th row: P6, Tw4R, [P1, K1] twice, P2.
20th row: As 6th row.
21st row: P4, Tw4R, [P1, K1] 3 times, P2.
22nd row: As 4th row.
23rd row: P2, Tw4R, [P1, K1] 4 times, P2.
24th row: As 2nd row.
These 24 rows form patt.

PANEL B
Worked over 12 sts.
1st row (right side): P2, K8, P2.
2nd row and 2 foll alt rows: K2, P8, K2.
3rd row: P2, C4B, C4F, P2.
5th row: As 1st row.
7th row: P2, C4F, C4B, P2.
8th row: As 2nd row.
These 8 rows form patt.

PANEL C
Worked over 30 sts.
1st row (right side): P4, Cr3R, P5, sl next 3 sts onto cable needle and leave at back of work, K3, then K3 from cable needle, P5, Cr3L, P4.
2nd row: K4, P2, K6, P6, K6, P2, K4.
3rd row: P3, Cr3R, P4, Cr5R, Cr5L, P4, Cr3L, P3.
4th row: K3, P2, K5, P3, K4, P3, K5, P2, K3.
5th row: P2, Cr3R, P3, Cr5R, P4, Cr5L, P3, Cr3L, P2.
6th row: K2, P2, K1, MB, K2, P3, K8, P3, K2, MB, K1, P2, K2.
7th row: P2, Cr3L, P3, K3, P8, K3, P3, Cr3R, P2.
8th row: K3, P2, K3, P3, K8, P3, K3, P2, K3.
9th row: P3, Cr3L, P2, Cr5L, P4, Cr5R, P2, Cr3R, P3.
10th row: K4, P2, [K4, P3] twice, K4, P2, K4.
11th row: P4, Cr3L, P3, Cr5L, Cr5R, P3, Cr3R, P4.
12th row: K3, MB, K1, P2, K5, P6, K5, P2, K1, MB, K3.
These 12 rows form patt.

PANEL D
Worked over 16 sts.
1st row (right side): P2, [K1, P1] 5 times, K2, P2.
2nd row: K2, P2, [K1, P1] 5 times, K2.
3rd row: P2, [K1, P1] 4 times, Cr4R, P2.
4th row: K4, P2, [K1, P1] 4 times, K2.
5th row: P2, [K1, P1] 3 times, Cr4R, P4.
6th row: K6, P2, [K1, P1] 3 times, K2.
7th row: P2, [K1, P1] twice, Cr4R, P6.
8th row: K8, P2, [K1, P1] twice, K2.
9th row: P2, K1, P1, Cr4R, P8.
10th row: K10, P2, K1, P1, K2.
11th row: P2, Cr4R, P3, MK, P6.
12th row: K12, P2, K2.
13th row: P2, K2, P2, MK, P5, MK, P3.
14th row: As 12th row.
15th row: P2, Tw4L, P3, MK, P6.
16th row: As 10th row.
17th row: P2, K1, P1, Tw4L, P4, MK, P3.
18th row: As 8th row.
19th row: P2, [K1, P1] twice, Tw4L, P6.
20th row: As 6th row.
21st row: P2, [K1, P1] 3 times, Tw4L, P4.
22nd row: As 4th row.
23rd row: P2, [K1, P1] 4 times, Tw4L, P2.
24th row: As 2nd row.
These 24 rows form patt.

SWEATER

BACK AND FRONT (alike)
With 3¼mm (No 10/US 3) needles cast on 109(115:121) sts.
Work rib patt as follows:
1st row (right side): K.
2nd row: P2, [K2, P4] to last 5 sts, K2, P3.
3rd row: K2, [Tw2L, K4] to last 5 sts, Tw2L, K3.
4th row: P2, [K1, P1, K1, P3] to last 5 sts, K1, P1, K1, P2.
5th row: K3, [Tw2L, K4] to last 4 sts, Tw2L, K2.
6th row: P3, [K2, P4] to last 4 sts, K2, P2.
7th row: K.
8th row: As 6th row.
9th row: K3, [Tw2R, K4] to last 4 sts, Tw2R, K2.
10th row: As 4th row.
11th row: K2, [Tw2R, K4] to last 5 sts, Tw2R, K3.
12th row: As 2nd row.
These 12 rows form rib patt. Work a further 7 rows in rib patt.
Inc row: Patt 7(9:7), M1, [patt 6(7:9), M1] to last 6(8:6) sts, patt to end [126(130:134) sts].
Change to 4½mm (No 7/US 7) needles.
Work patt as follows:
1st row (right side): [K1, P1] 4(5:6) times, K4, work 1st row of Panel A, K4, work 1st row of Panel B, K4, work 1st row of Panel C, K4, work 1st row of Panel B, K4, work 1st row of Panel D, K4, [P1, K1] 4(5:6) times.
2nd row: [P1, K1] 4(5:6) times, P4, work 2nd row of Panel D, P4, work 2nd row of Panel B, P4, work 2nd row of Panel C, P4, work 2nd row of Panel B, P4, work 2nd row of Panel A, P4, [K1, P1] 4(5:6) times.
3rd row: [P1, K1] 3(4:5) times, P2, C4F, work 3rd row of Panel A, C4F, work 3rd row of Panel B, C4F, work 3rd row of Panel C, C4B, work 3rd row of Panel B, C4B, work 3rd row of Panel D, C4B, P2, [K1, P1] 3(4:5) times.
4th row: [K1, P1] 3(4:5) times, K2, P4, work 4th row of Panel D, P4, work 4th row of Panel B, P4, work 4th row of Panel C, P4, work 4th row of Panel B, P4, work 4th row of Panel A, P4, K2, [P1, K1] 3(4:5) times.
These 4 rows set position of Panels and form double moss st patt at side edges.
Cont in patt as set until work measures 45(48:52)cm/17¾ (19:20½)in from beg, ending with a wrong side row.
Shape Shoulders
Cast off 24(24:25) sts at beg of next 2 rows and 24(25:26) sts at beg of foll 2 rows.
Leave rem 30(32:32) sts on a holder.

SLEEVES
With 3¼mm (No 10/US 3) needles cast on 43 sts.
Work 17 rows in rib patt as given for Back and Front welt.
Inc row: [Rib 1, M1] twice, [rib 2, M1, rib 1, M1] 13 times, rib 1, M1, rib 1 [72 sts].
Change to 4½mm (No 7/US 7) needles.
Work patt as follows:
1st row (right side): P1, K4, work 1st row of Panel B, K4, work 1st row of Panel C, K4, work 1st row of Panel B, K4, P1.
2nd row: K1, P4, work 2nd row of Panel B, P4, work 2nd row of Panel C, P4, work 2nd row of Panel B, P4, K1.
3rd row: P1, C4F, work 3rd row of Panel B, C4F, work 3rd row of Panel C, C4B, work 3rd row of Panel B, C4B, P1.
4th row: K1, P4, work 4th row of Panel B, P4, work 4th row of Panel C, P4, work 4th row of Panel B, P4, K1.
These 4 rows set position of Panels. Cont in patt as set, inc 1 st at each end of next row and every foll 6th(7th:6th) row until there are 90(94:98) sts, working inc sts into double moss st patt. Cont straight until Sleeve measures 30(33:36)cm/11¾ (13:14¼)in from beg, ending with a wrong side row.

Bobbles and Waves Sweater with Bag

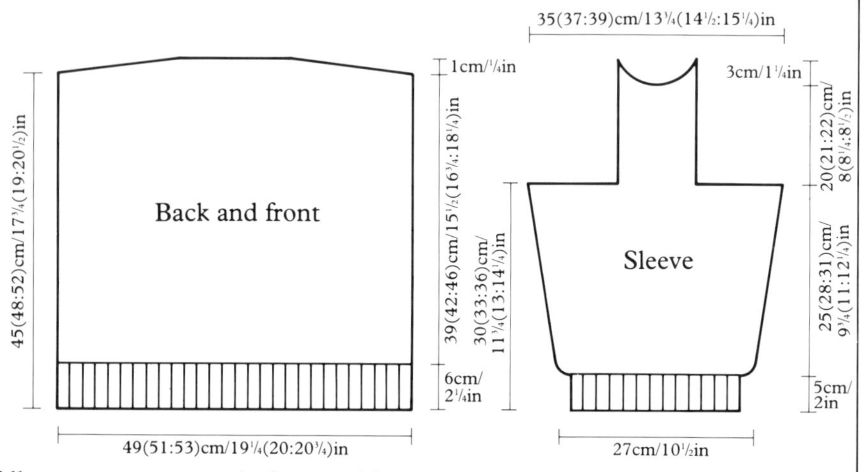

35(37:39)cm/13¾(14½:15¼)in
1cm/¼in
3cm/1¼in
45(48:52)cm/17¾(19:20½)in
Back and front
39(42:46)cm/15½(16¾:18¼)in
30(33:36)cm/11¾(13:14¼)in
Sleeve
20(21:22)cm/8(8¼:8¾)in
25(28:31)cm/9¾(11:12¼)in
6cm/2¼in
5cm/2in
49(51:53)cm/19¼(20:20¾)in
27cm/10½in

All measurements are before washing

Shape Saddle
Cast off 30(32:34) sts at beg of next 2 rows. Cont in patt on rem 30 sts for 20(21:22)cm/8(8¼:8½)in, ending with a wrong side row.
Shape Neck
Next row: Patt 8, work 2 tog, turn. Work on this set of sts only. Keeping patt correct, dec 1 st at inside edge on every row until 2 sts rem. Work 2 tog and fasten off.
With right side facing, slip centre 10 sts onto a holder, rejoin yarn to rem sts, work 2 tog, patt to end. Complete to match first side.

NECKBAND
With 3¼mm (No 10/US 3) needles and right side facing, pick up and K9 sts down first inside edge of left sleeve saddle, K centre sts, pick up and K9 sts up second side, K across centre front sts dec 0(2:2) sts evenly across, pick up and K9 sts down first inside edge of right sleeve saddle, K centre sts, pick up and K9 sts up second side, then K across centre back sts dec 1(3:3) sts evenly across [115 sts].
Beg with a 2nd row, work 19 rows in rib patt as given for Back and Front welt. Beg with a K row, work 6 rows in st st. Cast off.
Join neckband seam, reversing seam on st st section.

TO MAKE UP
Wash the pieces according to the instructions given on ball band. Join saddles to shoulders of back and front, then sew on remaining sleeve tops. Join side and sleeve seams.

BAG
TO MAKE
With 4mm (No 8/US 6) needles cast on 112 sts. Work in garter st (every row K) for 32cm/12½in. Cast off 52 sts at beg of next 2 rows. Cont in garter st on rem 8 sts for 56cm/22in for strap. Cast off. Fold bag in half widthwise and join side and bottom seam. Sew cast off edge of strap to side seam.

Tree of Life Guernsey page 31

MATERIALS
10 50g balls of Rowan DK Handknit Cotton.
Pair each of 3¼mm (No 10/US 3) and 4mm (No 8/US 6) knitting needles.
Cable needle.
3 buttons.

MEASUREMENTS

To fit age	3–4 years
Actual chest measurement	86 cm 34 in
Length	49 cm 19¼in
Sleeve seam	30 cm 11¼in

TENSION
20 sts and 28 rows to 10cm/4in square over st st on 4mm (No 8/US 6) needles.

ABBREVIATIONS
See page 42.

PANEL A
Worked over 13 sts.
1st row (right side): K1, P11, K1.
2nd row: P1, K11, P1.
3rd row: As 1st row.
4th row: P13.
5th row: K13.
6th row: P6, K1, P6.
7th row: K5, P1, K1, P1, K5.
8th row: P4, K1, [P1, K1] twice, P4.
9th row: K3, P1, [K1, P1] 3 times, K3.
10th row: P2, K1, [P1, K1] 4 times, P2.
11th row: K1, [P1, K1] 6 times.
12th row: As 10th row.
13th row: As 9th row.
14th row: As 8th row.
15th row: As 7th row.
16th row: As 6th row.
17th row: K13.
18th row: P13.
These 18 rows form patt.

PANEL B
Worked over 9 sts.
1st row (right side): K1, P7, K1.
2nd row: P1, K7, P1.
3rd row: As 1st row.
4th row: P5, K2, P2.
5th row: K3, P2, K4.
6th row: P3, K2, P4.
7th row: K5, P2, K2.
8th row: P1, K2, P6.
9th row: K6, P2, K1.
10th row: P2, K2, P5.
11th row: K4, P2, K3.
12th row: P4, K2, P3.
13th row: K2, P2, K5.
14th row: P6, K2, P1.
15th row: K1, P2, K6.
Rows 4th to 15th form patt.

PANEL C
Worked over 4 sts.
1st row (right side): K4.
2nd row: P4.
3rd row: Sl next 2 sts onto cable needle and leave at front of work, K2, then K2 from cable needle.
4th row: P4.
5th and 6th rows: As 1st and 2nd rows.
These 6 rows form patt.

PANEL D
Worked over 15 sts.
1st row (right side): K1, P13, K1.
2nd row: P1, K13, P1.

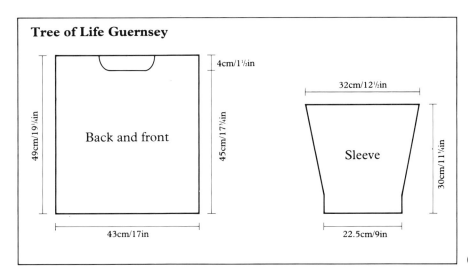

Tree of Life Guernsey

Back and front — 49cm/19¼in, 43cm/17in, 45cm/17¾in, 4cm/1½in

Sleeve — 32cm/12½in, 30cm/11¼in, 22.5cm/9in

3rd row: K1, P13, K1.
4th row: P15.
5th row: K15.
6th row: P7, K1, P7.
7th row: K6, P1, K1, P1, K6.
8th row: P5, K1, P3, K1, P5.
9th row: K4, P1, [K2, P1] twice, K4.
10th row: P3, K1, P2, K1, P1, K1, P2, K1, P3.
11th row: [K2, P1] twice, K3, [P1, K2] twice.
12th row: P4, K1, [P2, K1] twice, P4.
13th row: K3, P1, K2, P1, K1, P1, K2, P1, K3.
14th row: As 8th row.
15th row: As 9th row.
16th row: P6, K1, P1, K1, P6.
17th row: K5, P1, K3, P1, K5.
18th row: As 6th row.
19th row: K6, P3, K6.
20th row: As 6th row.
21st row: K15.
22nd row: P15.
These 22 rows form patt.

BACK

With 3¼mm (No 10/US 3) needles cast on 86 sts.
Beg with a K row, work 6 rows in st st.
1st row (right side): K2, [P2, K2] to end.
2nd row: P2, [K2, P2] to end.
Rep last 2 rows twice more.
Change to 4mm (No 8/US 6) needles.
Beg with a K row, work in st st until Back measures 9cm/3½in from beg, ending with a P row and inc 5 sts evenly across last row [91 sts].
Work main patt as follows:
Next row: P1, K1, P1, work 1st row of Panel A, P1, K1, P1, work 1st row of Panel B, P1, K1, P1, work 1st row of Panel C, P1, K1, P1, work 1st row of Panel D, P1, K1, P1, work 1st row of Panel C, P1, K1, P1, work 1st row of Panel B, P1, K1, P1, work 1st row of Panel A, P1, K1, P1.
This row sets position of Panels and form moss st patt between Panels.
Work a further 107 rows. **
Now work yoke patt as follows: P 1 row.
*** K 1 row. P 2 rows. K 2 rows. P 1 row.
K 2 rows. P 1 row. K 1 row. P 1 row.
Leave sts on a spare needle.

FRONT

Work as given for Back to **.
Shape Neck
Next row: P37, turn.
Work on this set of sts only. Work in yoke patt as given for Back from ***, **at the same time**, dec 1 st at neck edge on next 10 rows [27 sts]. Leave these sts on a holder.
With right side facing, sl centre 17 sts onto a holder, rejoin yarn to rem sts and P to end. Complete to match first side.

SLEEVES

With 3¼mm (No 10/US 3) needles cast on 38 sts.
Beg with a K row, work 6 rows in st st, then work in rib as given for Back until Sleeve measures 5cm/2in from beg, ending with a wrong side row and inc 7 sts evenly across last row [45 sts].
Change to 4mm (No 8/US 6) needles.
Beg with a K row, work 36 rows in st st, **at the same time**, inc 1 st at each end of every foll 5th row [59 sts].
Work main patt as follows:
Next row: P1, K1, P1, work 1st row of Panel B, P1, K1, P1, work 1st row of Panel C, P1, K1, P1, work 1st row of Panel D, P1, K1, P1, work 1st row of Panel C, P1, K1, P1, work 1st row of Panel B, P1, K1, P1.

This row sets position of Panels and forms moss st patt between Panels.
Cont in patt as set for a further 35 rows, **at the same time**, inc 1 st at each end of 4th row and 4 foll 6th rows, working inc sts into moss st patt [69 sts]. Cast off.

NECKBAND

Graft 27 sts at right side of back with right side of front sts for right shoulder seam.
With 3¼mm (No 10/US 3) needles and right side facing, pick up and K22 sts down left front neck, K centre front sts, pick up and K22 sts up right front neck, K37 sts from back neck, turn and cast on 4 sts for button band [102 sts]. K 1 row. P 2 rows.
1st row: K6, [P2, K2] to last 4 sts, K4.
2nd row: K4, [P2, K2] to last 6 sts, P2, K4.

3rd row (buttonhole): K1, K2 tog, yf, K3, [P2, K2] to last 4 sts, K4.
4th row: As 2nd row.
5th and 6th rows: As 1st and 2nd rows.
Rep last 6 rows once more. K 1 row.
Next row: K4, P to last 4 sts, K4.
Buttonhole row: K1, K2 tog, yf, K to end.
Next row: K4, P to last 4 sts, K4.
Cast off knitwise.

TO MAKE UP

Graft left shoulder seam. Catch down cast on edge of button band behind buttonhole band on neckband. Sew on buttons. Sew on sleeves, beginning and ending 33cm/13in from cast on edge of back and front. Join side and sleeve seams.

Cotton Aran Sweater page 32

MATERIALS

11(12:12) 50g balls of Rowan DK Handknit Cotton.
Pair each of 3¼mm (No 10/US 3) and 4mm (No 8/US 6) knitting needles.
Cable needle.

MEASUREMENTS

To fit age	2–3	4–5	5–6 years
Actual chest measurement	89 35	93 36½	97 cm 38 in
Length	44 17¼	46 18	48 cm 19 in
Sleeve seam	25 10	27 10½	30 cm 11¾in

TENSION

20 sts and 28 rows to 10cm/4in square over st st on 4mm (No 8/US 6) needles.

ABBREVIATIONS

Cr3L = sl next 2 sts onto cable needle and leave at front of work, P1, then K2 from cable needle;
Cr3R = sl next st onto cable needle and leave at back of work, K2, then P st from cable needle;

C4B = sl next 2 sts onto cable needle and leave at back of work, K2, then K2 from cable needle;
C4F = sl next 2 sts onto cable needle and leave at front of work, K2, then K2 from cable needle;
MB = make bobble as follows: pick up loop lying between st just work and next st and work K1, P1, K1 and P1 into it, turn, P4, turn, k4 tog;
Tw3L = sl next 2 sts onto cable needle and leave at front of work, P1, then K2 tbl from cable needle;
Tw3R = sl next st onto cable needle and leave at back of work, K2 tbl, then P st from cable needle;
T4B = sl next 2 sts onto cable needle and leave at back of work, K2 tbl, then K2 tbl from cable needle;
T4F = sl next 2 sts onto cable needle and leave at front of work, K2 tbl, then K2 tbl from cable needle.
Also see page 42.

70

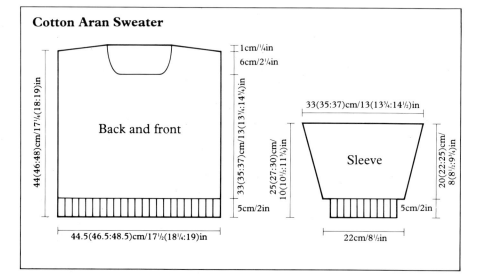

Cotton Aran Sweater

Back and front
44(46:48)cm/17¼(18:19)in
44.5(46.5:48.5)cm/17½(18¼:19)in
33(35:37)cm/13(13¼:14½)in
1cm/¼in
6cm/2¼in

Sleeve
33(35:37)cm/13(13¼:14½)in
25(27:30)cm/10(10½:11¾)in
5cm/2in
20(22:25)cm/8(8½:9¾)in
22cm/8½in
5cm/2in

PANEL A
Worked over 11 sts.
1st row (wrong side): K7, P2, K2.
2nd row: P2, Cr3L, P6.
3rd row: K6, P2, K3.
4th row: P2, K1, Cr3L, P5.
5th row: K5, P2, K1, P1, K2.
6th row: P3, K1, Cr3L, P4.
7th row: K4, P2, K1, P1, K3.
8th row: P2, K1, P1, K1, Cr3L, P3.
9th row: K3, P2, [K1, P1] twice, K2.
10th row: P3, K1, P1, K1, Cr3L, P2.
11th row: K2, P2, [K1, P1] twice, K3.
12th row: P2, [K1, P1] twice, Cr3R, P2.
13th row: As 9th row.
14th row: P3, K1, P1, Cr3R, P3.
15th row: As 7th row.
16th row: P2, K1, P1, Cr3R, P4.
17th row: As 5th row.
18th row: P3, Cr3R, P5.
19th row: As 3rd row.
20th row: P2, Cr3R, P2, MB, P1, then pass bobble st over the P st, P3.
These 20 rows form patt.

PANEL B
Worked over 12 sts.
1st row and every foll alt row (wrong side): K2, P8, K2.
2nd row: P2, C4B, C4F, P2.
4th row: P2, K8, P2.
6th row: P2, C4F, C4B, P2.
8th row: P2, K8, P2.
These 8 rows form patt.

PANEL C
Worked over 32 sts.
1st row (wrong side): K7, P4, K10, P4, K7.
2nd row: P7, T4F, P5, MB, P1, then pass bobble st over the P st, P4, T4F, P7.
3rd row: As 1st row.
4th row: P6, Tw3R, Tw3L, P8, Tw3R, Tw3L, P6.
5th row: K6, P3, K1, P2, K8, P3, K1, P2, K6.
6th row: P5, Tw3R, K1, P1, Tw3L, P6, Tw3R, K1, P1, Tw3L, P5.
7th row: K5, P3, K1, P1, K1, P2, K6, P3, K1, P1, K1, P2, K5.
8th row: P4, Tw3R, [K1, P1] twice, Tw3L, P4, Tw3R, [K1, P1] twice, Tw3L, P4.
9th row: K4, P2, [K1, P1] 3 times, P2, K4, P2, [K1, P1] 3 times, P2, K4.
10th row: P3, Tw3R, [K1, P1] 3 times, Tw3L, P2, Tw3R, [K1, P1] 3 times, Tw3L, P3.
11th row: K3, P2, [K1, P1] 4 times, P2, K2, P2, [K1, P1] 4 times, P2, K3.
12th row: P2, Tw3R, [K1, P1] 4 times, Tw3L, Tw3R, [K1, P1] 4 times, Tw3L, P2.
13th row: K2, P2, [K1, P1] 5 times, P4, [K1, P1] 5 times, P2, K2.
14th row: P2, K2 tbl, [K1, P1] 5 times, T4F, [K1, P1] 5 times, K2 tbl, P2.
15th row: K2, P2, [K1, P1] 5 times, P4, [K1, P1] 5 times, P2, K2.
16th row: P2, Tw3L, [K1, P1] 4 times, Tw3R, Tw3L, [K1, P1] 4 times, Tw3R, P2.
17th row: K3, P2, [K1, P1] 4 times, P2, K2, P2, [K1, P1] 4 times, P2, K3.
18th row: P3, Tw3L, [K1, P1] 3 times, Tw3R, P2, Tw3L, [K1, P1] 3 times, Tw3R, P3.
19th row: K4, P2, [K1, P1] 3 times, P2, K4, P2, [K1, P1] 3 times, P2, K4.
20th row: P4, Tw3L, [K1, P1] twice, Tw3R, P4, Tw3L, [K1, P1] twice, Tw3R, P4.
21st row: K5, P2, [K1, P1] twice, P2, K6, P2, [K1, P1] twice, P2, K5.

22nd row: P5, Tw3L, K1, P1, Tw3R, P6, Tw3L, K1, P1, Tw3R, P5.
23rd row: K6, P2, K1, P3, K8, P2, K1, P3, K6.
24th row: P6, Tw3L, Tw3R, P8, Tw3L, Tw3R, P6.
These 24 rows form patt.

PANEL D
Worked over 11 sts.
1st row (wrong side): K2, P2, K7.
2nd row: P6, Cr3R,. P2.
3rd row: K3, P2, K6.
4th row: P5, Cr3R, K1, P2.
5th row: K2, P1, K1, P2, K5.
6th row: P4, Cr3R, K1, P3.
7th row: K3, P1, K1, P2, K4.
8th row: P3, Cr3R, K1, P1, K1, P2.
9th row: K2, [P1, K1] twice, P2, K3.
10th row: P2, Cr3R, K1, P1, K1, P3.
11th row: K3, [P1, K1] twice, P2, K2.
12th row: P2, Cr3L, [P1, K1] twice, P2.
13th row: As 9th row.
14th row: P3, Cr3L, P1, K1, P3.
15th row: As 7th row.
16th row: P4, Cr3L, P1, K1, P2.
17th row: As 5th row.
18th row: P5, Cr3L, P3.
19th row: As 3rd row.
20th row: P4, MB, P1, then pass bobble st over the P st, P1, Cr3L, P2.
These 20 rows form patt.

BACK
With 3¼mm (No 10/US 3) needles cast on 104(108:112) sts.
1st row (wrong side): K2(1:3), [P1 tb1, K2] 1(2:2) times, * P4, K2, [P1 tb1, K2] 3 times *; rep from * to * once, P4, K2, [P1 tb1, K2] 8 times, rep from * to * twice, P4, [K2, P1 tb1] 1(2:2) times, K2(1:3).
2nd row: P2(1:3), [K1 tb1, P2] 1(2:2) times, *C4F, P2, [K1 tb1, P2] 3 times; rep from * once, C4F, P2, [K1 tb1, P2] 8 times, C4B, ** P2, [K1 tb1, P2] 3 times, C4B; rep from ** once, [P2, K1 tb1] 1(2:2) times, P2(1:3).
3rd row: As 1st row.
4th row: P2(1:3), [K1 tb1, P2] 1(2:2) times, * K4, P2, [K1 tb1, P2] 3 times *; rep from * to * once, K4, P2, [K1 tb1, P2] 8 times, rep from * to * twice, K4, [P2, K1 tb1] 1(2:2) times, P2(1:3).
Rep 1st to 4th rows twice more, then work 1st row again.
Inc row: Patt 2(4:6), M1, patt 2, M1, patt 25, Ml, patt 12, M1, patt 3, M1, [patt 5, M1] 3 times, patt 4, M1, patt 12, M1, patt 25, M1, patt 2, M1, patt 2(4:6) [116(120:124) sts].
Change to 4mm (No 8/US 6) needles.
Work patt as follows:
1st row (wrong side): [K1, P1] 2(3:4) times, K3, P4, work 1st row of Panel A, P4, work 1st row of Panel B, P4, work 1st row of Panel C, P4, work 1st row of Panel B, P4, work 1st row of Panel D, P4, K3, [P1, K1] 2(3:4) times.
2nd row: [P1, K1] 2(3:4) times, P3, K4, work 2nd row of Panel D, K4, work 2nd row of Panel B, K4, work 2nd row of Panel C, K4, work 2nd row of Panel B, K4, work 2nd row of Panel A, K4, P3, [K1, P1] 2(3:4) times.
3rd row: [P1, K1] 3(4:5) times, K1, P4, work 3rd row of Panel A, P4, work 3rd row of Panel B, P4, work 3rd row of Panel C, P4, work 3rd row of Panel B, P4, work 3rd row of Panel D, P4, K1, [K1, P1] 3(4:5) times.
4th row: [K1, P1] 3(4:5) times, P1, C4F, work 4th row of Panel D, C4F, work 4th row of Panel B, C4F, work 4th row of Panel C, C4B, work 4th row of Panel B, C4B, work 4th row of Panel A, C4B, P1, [P1, K1] 3(4:5) times.
These 4 rows set position of Panels and form double moss st patt at side edges.
Cont in patt as set until work measures 44(46:48)cm/17¼(18:19)in from beg, ending with a wrong side row.
Shape Shoulders
Cast off 18(18:19) sts at beg of next 2 rows and 18(19:19) sts at beg of foll 2 rows.
Leave rem 44(46:48) sts on a holder.

FRONT
Work as given for Back until Front measures 38(40:42)cm/15(15¾:16¾)in from beg, ending with a wrong side row.
Shape Neck
Next row: Patt 48(49:50), turn.
Work on this set of sts only. Keeping patt correct, dec 1 st at neck edge on every row until 36(37:38) sts rem. Cont straight until Front matches Back to shoulder shaping, ending at side edge.
Shape Shoulders
Cast off 18(18:19) sts at beg of next row. Work 1 row. Cast off rem 18(19:19) sts.
With right side facing, slip centre 20 (22:24) sts onto a holder, rejoin yarn to rem sts and patt to end. Complete to match first side.

SLEEVES
With 3¼mm (No 10/US 3) needles cast on 47 sts.
1st row (wrong side): K2, P1 tb1, K2, P4, K2, [P1 tb1, K2] 9 times, P4, K2, P1 tb1, K2.
2nd row: P2, K1 tb1, P2, C4F, P2, [K1 tb1, P2] 9 times, C4B, P2, K1 tb1, P2.
3rd row: As 1st row.
4th row: P2, K1 tb1, P2, K4, P2, [K1 tb1, P2] 9 times, K4, P2, K1 tb1, P2.
Rep 1st to 4th rows twice more, then work 1st row again.
Inc row: [Patt 2, M1] twice, patt 7, M1, [patt 12, M1] twice, patt 8, [M1, patt 2] twice [54 sts].
Change to 4mm (No 8/US 6) needles.
Work patt as follows:
1st row (wrong side): [K1, P1] twice, K3, P4, work 1st row of Panel C, P4, K3, [P1, K1] twice.
2nd row: [P1, K1] twice, P3, K4, work 2nd row of Panel C, K4, P3, [K1, P1] twice.
3rd row: [P1, K1] 3 times, K1, P4, work 3rd row of Panel C, P4, K1, [K1, P1] 3 times.
4th row: [K1, P1] 3 times, P1, C4F, work 4th row of Panel C, C4B, P1, [P1, K1] 3 times.
These 4 rows set position of Panels and form double moss st patt at side edges.
Cont in patt as set, **at the same time**, inc

1 st at each end of next row and every foll 4th row until there are 76(80:84) sts, working inc sts into double moss st patt. Cont straight until Sleeve measures 25(27:30)cm/10(10½:11¾)in from beg, ending with a wrong side row. Cast off.

NECKBAND
Join right shoulder seam.
With 3¼mm (No 10/US 3) needles and right side facing, pick up and K9 sts down left front neck to 4-st cable, 4 sts across cable, 6 sts along rem left front neck, K across centre front neck sts, dec 3 sts evenly, pick up and K6 sts up right front neck to 4-st cable, 4 sts across cable, then 9 sts to shoulder, K centre back neck sts, dec 2 sts evenly [97(101:105) sts].
1st row (wrong side): K1, [P1 tb1, K1] 25(26:27) times, P4, K1, [P1 tb1, K1] 14(15:16) times, P4, K1, [P1 tb1, K1] 4 times.
2nd row: P1, [K1 tb1, P1] 4 times, K4, P1, [K1 tb1, P1] 14(15:16) times, K4, P1, [K1 tb1, P1] 25(26:27) times.
3rd row: As 1st row
4th row: P1, [K1 tb1, P1] 4 times, C4F, P1, [K1 tb1, P1] 14(15:16) times, C4B, P1, [K1 tb1, P1] 25(26:27) times.
Rep 1st to 4th rows twice more, then work 1st row again. Cast off in patt.

TO MAKE UP
Join left shoulder and neckband seam. Sew on sleeves, placing centre of sleeves to shoulder seams. Join side and sleeve seams.

Diamond and Moss Stitch Cardigan page 33

MATERIALS
10 50g balls of Rowan DK Handknit Cotton.
Pair each of 3¼mm (No 10/US 3) and 4mm (No 8/US 6) knitting needles.
6 buttons.

MEASUREMENTS

To fit age	2–4 years
Actual chest measurement	85 cm 33½in
Length	44 cm 17½in
Sleeve seam	25 cm 10 in

TENSION
20 sts and 28 rows to 10cm/4in square over st st on 4mm (No 8/US 6) needles.

ABBREVIATIONS
MK = make knot as follows: [P1, K1, P1, K1, P1] all in next st, then pass 2nd, 3rd, 4th and 5th sts over first st.
Also see page 42.

PANEL A
Worked over 5 sts.
1st row (right side): P5.
2nd row: K5.
3rd row: P2, MK, P2.
4th row: K5.
These 4 rows form patt.

PANEL B
Worked over 15 sts.
1st row (right side): K1, P13, K1.
2nd row: P1, K13, P1.
3rd row: As 1st row.
4th row: P15.
5th row: K15.
6th row: P15.
7th row: K7, P1, K7.
8th row: P6, K1, P1, K1, P6.
9th row: K5, P1, [K1, P1] twice, K5.
10th row: P4, K1, [P1, K1] 3 times, P4.
11th row: K3, P1, [K1, P1] 4 times, K3.
12th row: P2, K1, [P1, K1] 5 times, P2.
13th row: As 11th row.
14th row: As 10th row.
15th row: As 9th row.
16th row: As 8th row.
17th row: As 7th row.
18th row: P15.
19th row: K15.
20th row: P15.
These 20 rows form patt.

BACK
With 3¼mm (No 10/US 3) needles cast on 82 sts.
Beg with a K row, work 4 rows in st st.
Work rib patt as follows:
1st row (right side): K2, [P3, K2] to end.
2nd row: P2, [K3, P2] to end.

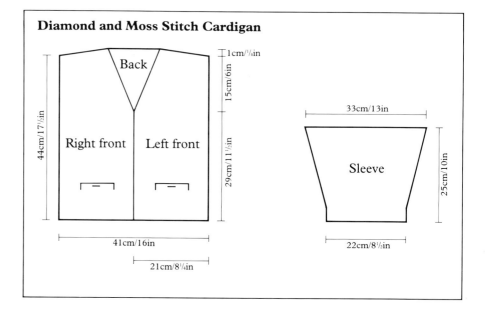

Diamond and Moss Stitch Cardigan

3rd row: K2, [P1, MK, P1, K2] to end.
4th row: As 2nd row.
These 4 rows form rib patt. Rep them once more.
Change to 4mm (No 8/US 6) needles.
Beg with a K row, work in st st until Back measures 14cm/5½in from beg, ending with a P row and inc 5 sts evenly across last row [87 sts].
Work main patt as follows:
1st row: P1, [work 1st row of Panel A, then Panel B] 4 times, work 1st row of Panel A, P1.
2nd row: K1, [work 2nd row of Panel A, then Panel B] 4 times, work 2nd row of Panel A, K1.
These 2 rows set position of Panels. Cont in patt as set until Back measures 44cm/17½in from beg, ending with a wrong side row.
Shape Shoulders
Cast off 13 sts at beg of next 2 rows and 14 sts at beg of foll 2 rows. Leave rem 33 sts on a holder.

POCKET LININGS (make 2)
With 4mm (No 8/US 6) needles cast on 17 sts. Work 9cm/3½in in st st, ending with a K row. Leave these sts on a holder.

LEFT FRONT
With 3¼mm (No 10/US 3) needles cast on 42 sts.
Beg with a K row, work 4 rows in st st, then work 8 rows in rib patt as given for Back.
Change to 4mm (No 8/US 6) needles.
Next row (right side): K14, [P1, K1] 8 times, K12.
Next row: P12, [K1, P1] 8 times, K1, P13.
Rep last 2 rows until Front measures 11cm/4¼in from beg, ending with a wrong side row.
Buttonhole row: Patt 21, yrn, P2 tog, patt 19.
Work 3 rows in patt.
Next row: K13, cast off next 17 sts, K to end.
Next row: P12, P across sts of first pocket lining, P13.
Cont in st st for a few rows until Front measures 14cm/5½in from beg, ending with a P row and inc 1 st at centre of last row [43 sts].
Work main patt as follows:
1st row: P1, [work 1st row of Panel A, then Panel B] twice, P2.
2nd row: K2, [work 2nd row of Panel B, then Panel A] twice, K1.
These 2 rows set position of Panels. Cont in patt as set until Front measures 29cm/11½in from beg, ending with a wrong side row.
Shape Neck
Keeping patt correct, dec 1 st at neck edge on next row, 3 foll alt rows, then on every foll 3rd row until 27 sts rem. Cont straight for a few rows until Front matches Back to shoulder shaping, ending at side edge.
Shape Shoulder
Cast off 13 sts at beg of next row. Work 1 row. Cast off rem 14 sts.

RIGHT FRONT
With 3¼mm (No 10/US 3) needles cast on 42 sts.
Beg with a K row, work 4 rows in st st, then work 8 rows in rib patt as given for Back.
Change to 4mm (No 8/US 6) needles.
Next row (right side): K13, [P1, K1] 8 times, K13.

Next row: P13, K1, [P1, K1] 8 times, P12.
Rep last 2 rows until Front measures 11cm/4¼in from beg, ending with a wrong side row.
Buttonhole row: Patt 19, P2 tog, yrn, patt 21.
Work 3 rows in patt.
Next row: K12, cast off next 17 sts, K to end.
Next row: P13, P across sts of second pocket lining, P12.
Cont in st st for a few rows until Front measures 14cm/5½in from beg, ending with a P row and inc 1 st at centre of last row [43 sts].
Work main patt as follows:
1st row: P2, [work 1st row of Panel B, then Panel A] twice, P1.
2nd row: K1, [work 2nd row of Panel A, then Panel B] twice, K2.
These 2 rows set position of Panels.
Complete as given for Left Front.

SLEEVES
With 3¼mm (No 10/US 3) needles cast on 37 sts.
Beg with a K row, work 4 rows in st st, then work 8 rows in rib patt as given for Back and inc 8 sts evenly across last row [45 sts].
Change to 4mm (No 8/US 6) needles.
Work main patt as follows:
1st row: [Work 1st row of Panel A, then Panel B] twice, work 1st row of Panel A.
2nd row: [Work 2nd row of Panel A, then Panel B] twice, work 2nd row of Panel A.

These 2 rows set position of Panels. Cont in patt as set, inc 1 st at each end of next row, 5 foll 3rd rows, then on every 4th row until there are 71 sts, working inc sts into patt. Cont straight until Sleeve measures 25cm/10in from beg, ending with a wrong side row. Cast off.

FRONT BAND
With 3¼mm (No 10/US 3) needles and right side facing, pick up and K57 sts up front edge of Right Front, 35 sts up shaped edge to shoulder, K back neck sts, pick up and K35 sts down shaped edge of Left Front to beg of neck shaping and 57 sts along straight edge [217 sts].
Next row: P2, [K3, P2] to end.
1st buttonhole row: K2, P1, MK, P1, * cast off 2 (1 st on right hand needle), MK, P1, [K2, P1, MK, P1] twice; rep from * 3 times more, [K2, P1, MK, P1] to last 2 sts, K2.
2nd buttonhole row: [P2, K3] to last 44 sts, cast on 2 sts, * [K3, P2] twice, K3, cast on 2 sts; rep from * twice more, K3, P2.
Beg with a K row, work 4 rows in st st. Cast off.

TO MAKE UP
Sew on sleeves, placing centre of sleeves to shoulder seams. Join side and sleeve seams. Sew on 4 buttons to front band and one to each pocket lining.

"Star" Sweater with Sandals page 34

MATERIALS
Sweater: 4(5) 50g balls of Rowan Cotton Glace.
Pair each of 2¾mm (No 12/US 1), 3mm (No 11/US 2) and 3¼mm (No 10/US 3) knitting needles.
6 buttons.
Sandals: 1 50g ball of Rowan Cotton Glace.
Pair of 2¾mm (No 12/US 2) knitting needles.
Medium size crochet hook.
2 buttons.

MEASUREMENTS
Sweater:

To fit age	3–6	6–12 months
Actual chest measurement	60 23½	65 cm 25½in
Length	30 11¾	33 cm 13 in
Sleeve seam	16 6½	18 cm 7¼in

Sandals:

To fit age	3–12 months

TENSION
26 sts and 34 rows to 10cm/4in square over st st on 3¼mm (No 10/US 3) needles.

ABBREVIATIONS
See page 42.

NOTE
Read Chart from right to left on right side rows, and from left to right on wrong side rows.

SWEATER
FRONT
With 3mm (No 11/US 2) needles cast on 79(85) sts. K 6 rows.
Change to 3¼mm (No 10/US 3) needles.
Next row: K.
Next row: K3, P to last 3 sts, K3.
Rep last 2 rows twice more.
Beg with a K row, work in st st until Front measures 9(11)cm/3½(4¼)in from beg, ending with a P row.
Place star motif as follows:
1st row (right side): K28(31), work across 1st row of Chart, K28(31).

73

2nd row: P28(31), work across 2nd row of Chart, P28(31).
These 2 rows set position of star motif.
Work a further 31 rows as set.
Next row: P6, K5, P17(20), work across 34th row of Chart, P17(20), K5, P6.
Next row: K28(31), work across 35th row of Chart, K28(31).
Work a further 3 rows as set.
Next row: K.
Next row: P6, K5, P to last 11 sts, K5, P6.
Rep last 2 rows until Front measures 25(27)cm/10(10½)in from beg, ending with a wrong side row.

Shape Neck

Next row: Patt 24(26), turn.
Work on this set of sts only. Patt a further 5 rows.
Beg with a K row, cont in st st until Front measures 29(32)cm/11¾(12¼)in from beg, ending with a P row. Cast off.
With right side facing, slip centre 31(33) sts onto a holder, rejoin yarn to rem sts and patt to end. Complete to match first side.

BACK

Work as given for Front omitting star motif and shaping neck when work measures 27(29)cm/10¾(11¼)in from beg, ending with a wrong side row.

SLEEVES

With 2¾mm (No 12/US 1) needles cast on 42(46) sts.
1st row (right side): K2, [P2, K2] to end.
2nd row: P2, [K2, P2] to end.
Rep last 2 rows until Sleeve measures 3cm/1¼in from beg, ending with a right side row.
Inc row: Rib 2(4), inc in next st, [rib 3, inc in next st] to last 3(5) sts, rib 3(5) [52(56) sts].
Change to 3¼mm (No 10/US 3) needles.
Beg with a K row, work in st st inc 1 st at each end of every foll 3rd(4th) row until there are 62(66) sts. Cont straight until Sleeve measures 13(15)cm/5¼(6)in from beg, ending with a P row.
Now work 3cm/1¼in in rib as given for cuff, ending with a wrong side row. Cast off in rib.

BUTTONHOLE BANDS

With 3mm (No 11/US 2) needles and right side facing, pick up and K24(26) sts evenly along left front shoulder. K 1 row.
1st buttonhole row: K6, [cast off 2, K7(8) including st used in casting off] twice.
2nd buttonhole row: K to end, casting on 2 sts over those cast off in previous row.
K 2 rows. Cast off.
Work right front buttonhole band in same way, reversing buttonholes.

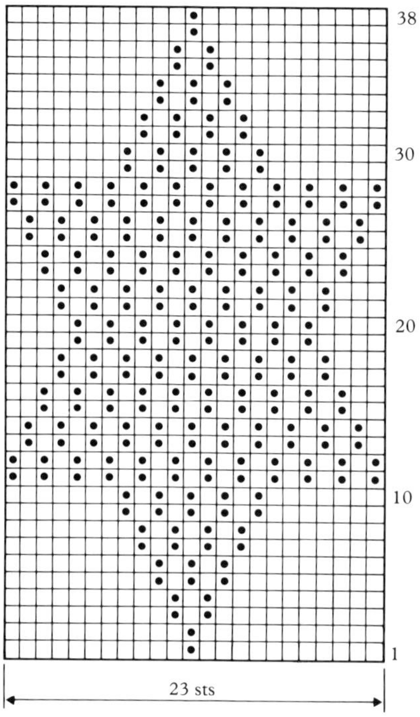

38
30
20
10
1
23 sts

KEY

☐ K on right side, P on wrong side

⊡ P on right side, K on wrong side

BUTTON BANDS

With 3mm (No 11/US 2) needles and right side facing, pick up K24(26) sts evenly along left back shoulder. K 5 rows. Cast off.
Work right back button band in same way.

BACK NECKBAND

With 3mm (No 11/US 2) needles and right side facing, pick up and K9 sts down right back neck, K centre back sts, pick up and K9 sts up left back neck [49(51) sts]. K1 row.
Dec row: K7, skpo, K2 tog, K27(29), skpo, K2 tog, K7.
K 1 row.
Dec row: K6, skpo, K2 tog, K25(27), skpo, K2 tog, K6.
K 1 row. Cast off, dec as before.

FRONT NECKBAND

With 3mm (No 11/US 2) needles and right side facing, pick up and K14 sts down left front neck, K centre front sts, pick up and K14 sts up right front neck [59(61) sts]. K 1 row.
1st buttonhole row: K2, cast off 2, K8 including st used in casting off, skpo, K2 tog, K27(29), skpo, K2 tog, K8, cast off 2, K to end.
2nd buttonhole row: K to end, casting on 2 sts over those cast off in previous row.
Dec row: K11, skpo, K2 tog, K25(27), skpo, K2 tog, K11.
K 1 row. Cast off, dec as before.

TO MAKE UP

Lap buttonhole bands over button bands and join row ends at side edges.
Sew on sleeves, placing centre of sleeves in line with buttonholes. Beginning 12 rows up from cast on edge, join side seams and sleeve seams. Sew on buttons.

SANDALS

LEFT SANDAL

With 2¾mm (No 12/US 2) needles cast on 36 sts. K 1 row.
1st row (wrong side): K1, yf, K16, [yf, K1] twice, yf, K16, yf, K1.
2nd row and 4 foll alt rows: K to end but working K tbl into yf of previous row.
3rd row: K2, yf, K16, yf, K3, yf, K2, yf, K16, yf, K2.
5th row: K3, yf, K16, [yf, K4] twice, yf, K16, yf, K3.
7th row: K4, yf, K16, yf, K6, yf, K5, yf, K16, yf, K4.
9th row: K5, yf, K16, [yf, K7] twice, yf, K16, yf, K5.
11th row: K22, yf, K9, yf, K8, yf, K22 [64 sts].
12th row: As 2nd row.
K 9 rows.

Shape Instep

Next row: K36, K2 tog, turn.
Next row: Sl 1, P8, P2 tog, turn.
Next row: Sl 1, K8, K2 tog, turn.
Rep last 2 rows 7 times more, then work the first of the 2 rows again.
Next row: Sl 1, K to end.
Next row: K17, K2 tog, P8, K2 tog, K17 [44 sts].
Next row: K24, turn.
Next row: P4, turn.
Next row: K4, turn.
Work in st st on these 4 sts only for 6cm/2¼in for front strap. Cast off.
With right side facing, rejoin yarn at base of strap, pick up and K12 sts along side edge of strap, turn and cast off knitwise all sts at this side of strap.
With right side facing, rejoin yarn to top of other side edge of strap, pick up and K12 sts along side edge of strap, then K rem 20 sts. Cast off knitwise.
Join sole and back seam. With 2¾mm (No 12/US 2) needles, right side facing and beginning and ending within 9 sts of back seam, pick up and K18 sts along back heel for ankle strap.
Next row: Cast on 4 sts, K to end, turn and cast on 22 sts [44 sts].
K 3 rows. Cast off. With crochet hook, make buttonhole loop at long end of ankle strap, sew on button to other end. Fold front strap over ankle strap to wrong side and slip stitch cast off edge in place.

RIGHT SANDAL

Work as given for Left Sandal, reversing cast on row on ankle strap.

'Star' Sweater with Sandals

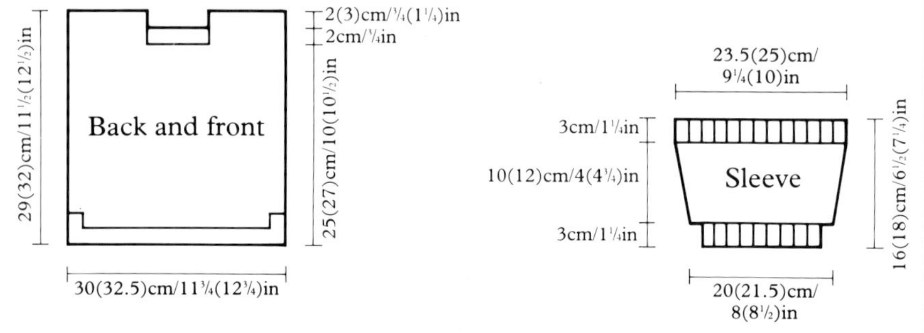

2(3)cm/¾(1¼)in
2cm/¾in
Back and front
29(32)cm/11½(12½)in
25(27)cm/10(10½)in
30(32.5)cm/11¾(12¾)in
23.5(25)cm/9¼(10)in
3cm/1¼in
10(12)cm/4(4¾)in
Sleeve
3cm/1¼in
16(18)cm/6½(7¼)in
20(21.5)cm/8(8½)in

Simple Guernsey Style Sweater page 35

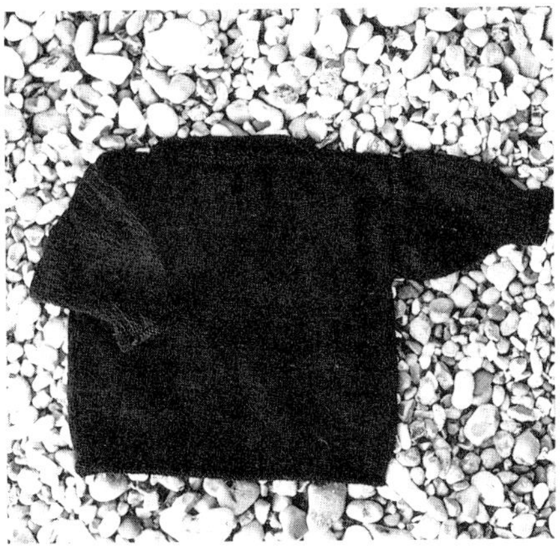

MATERIALS
7(7:8:9:10) 50g balls of Rowan DK Handknit Cotton.
Pair each of 3¼mm (No 10/US 3), 3¾mm (No 9/US 5) and 4mm (No 8/US 6) knitting needles.

MEASUREMENTS

To fit age	1-2	2-3	3-4	4-5	5-6 yrs
Actual chest	66	78	82	86	90 cm
measurement	26	30¾	32¼	34	35½in
Length	34	40	45	50	55 cm
	13½	15¾	17¾	19¾	21¾ in
Sleeve seam	18	21	24	27	30 cm
	7	8¼	9½	10¾	11¾in

TENSION
20 sts and 28 rows to 10cm/4in square over st st on 4mm (No 8/US 6) needles.

ABBREVIATIONS
See page 42.

BACK AND FRONT (alike)
With 3¾mm (No 9/US 5) needles cast on 66(78:82:86:90) sts.
Beg with a K row, work 6 rows in st st.
Next row (right side): K2, [P2, K2] to end.
Next row: P2, [K2, P2] to end.
Rep last 2 rows twice more.
Change to 4mm (No 8/US 6) needles.
Beg with a K row, cont in st st until work measures 18(23:27:31:35)cm/7(9:10½:12¼:13¾)in from beg, ending with a P row.
Work patt as follows:
Next row: K6, P5, K to last 11 sts, P5, K6.
Next row: P.
Rep last 2 rows until work measures 31(37:42:47:52)cm/12¼(14½:16½:18½:20½) in from beg, ending with a wrong side row.
Beg with a K row, cont in st st until work measures 34(40:45:50:55)cm/13½ (15¾:17¾:19¾:21¾)in from beg, ending with a P row. Cast off.

SLEEVES
With 3¼mm (No 10/US 3) needles cast on 34(34:38:38:42) sts.
Beg with a K row, work 6 rows in st st.
Next row (right side): K2, [P2, K2] to end.
Next row: P2, [K2, P2] to end.
Rep last 2 rows 4 times more, then work first of the 2 rows again.
Inc row: Rib 2(4:2:3:2), [inc in next st, rib 3(2:4:2:4), inc in next st, rib 3(2:3:3:4)] 4(5:4:5:4) times [42(44:46:48:50) sts].
Change to 4mm (No 8/US 6) needles.
Beg with a K row, work in st st, inc 1 st at each end of every foll 2nd(2nd:3rd:3rd:3rd) row until there are 66(70:74:78:82) sts.
Cont straight for a few rows until Sleeve measures 16(19:22:25:28)cm/6¼ (7½:8¾:10:11)in from beg, ending with a P row. Rep the 2 rows of rib 3 times. Cast off in rib.

NECKBAND
Join 14(19:20:21:22) sts at each side of back and front together for shoulder seams.
With 3¾mm (No 9/US 5) needles and right side facing, pick up and K40(42:44:46:48) sts along front neck edge. K 3 rows. Cast off knitwise.
With 3¾mm (No 9/US 5) needles and right side facing, pick up and K38(40:42:44:46) sts along back neck edge. K 6 rows, inc 1 st at each end of first row and foll alt row. Cast off knitwise.

TO MAKE UP
Fold front neckband to right side of work. Bring ends of back neckband over ends of front band and stitch sides together to front. Sew on sleeves, placing centre of sleeves to shoulder seams. Join side and sleeve seams, reversing seams on st st sections at hem and cuffs. Allow hem and cuffs to roll back.

Wee Willie Winkie Hat page 35

MATERIALS
3 50g balls of Rowan Designer DK Wool.
Pair each of 3¼mm (No 10/US 3) and 4mm (No 8/US 6) knitting needles.

MEASUREMENTS

To fit age	2-3 years
Length	80cm 31½in

TENSION
24 sts and 32 rows to 10cm/4in square over st st on 4mm (No 8/US 6) needles.

ABBREVIATIONS
See page 42.

TO MAKE
With 3¼mm (No 10/US 3) needles cast on 108 sts.
Work 7cm/2¾in in K2, P2 rib.
Change to 4mm (No 8/US 6) needles.
Beg with a K row, cont in st st until work measures 15cm/6in from beg, ending with a P row.
Dec row: [K25, K2 tog tbl, K2 tog, K25] twice.
Work 5 rows straight.
Dec row: [K24, K2 tog tbl, K2 tog, K24] twice.
Work 5 rows straight.
Dec row: [K23, K2 tog tbl, K2 tog, K23] twice.
Cont in this way, dec 4 sts as set on every 6th row until 64 sts rem, then 4 on foll 8th rows and 7 foll 12th rows [20 sts]. Cont straight until work measures 80cm/31½in from beg, ending with a P row. Break off yarn, thread end through rem sts, pull up and secure. Join seam. Make a large pompon and attach to point.

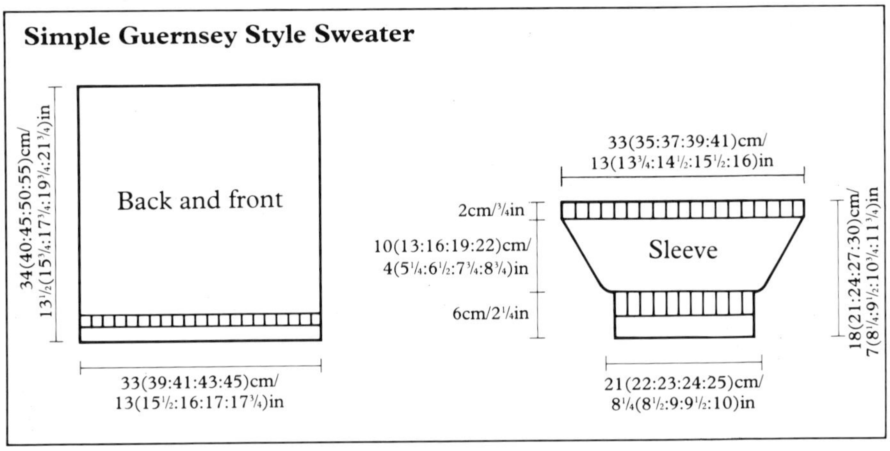
Simple Guernsey Style Sweater
34(40:45:50:55)cm/
13½(15¾:17¾:19¾:21¾)in
Back and front
33(39:41:43:45)cm/
13(15½:16:17:17¾)in
33(35:37:39:41)cm/
13(13¾:14½:15½:16)in
2cm/¾in
10(13:16:19:22)cm/
4(5¼:6½:7¾:8¾)in
Sleeve
6cm/2¼in
21(22:23:24:25)cm/
8¼(8½:9:9½:10)in
18(21:24:27:30)cm/
7(8¼:9½:10¾:11¾)in

Striped Tunic Top page 36

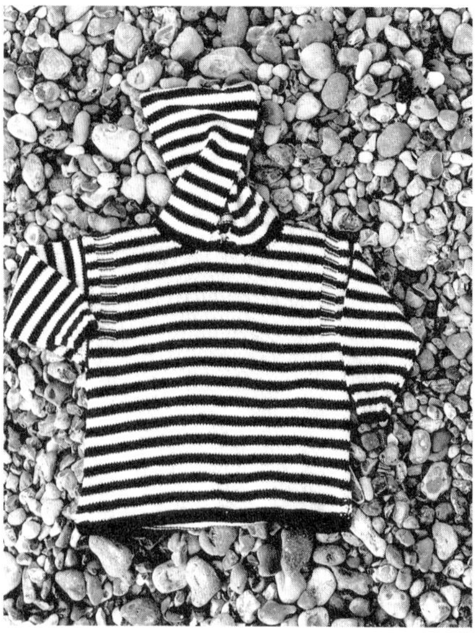

MATERIALS
4(5:5) 50g balls of Rowan Cotton Glace in both Navy (A) and White (B).
Pair each of 2¾mm (No 12/US 2) and 3¼mm (No 10/US 3) knitting needles.

MEASUREMENTS

To fit age	2	3	4 years
Actual chest measurement	71 28	76 30	81 cm 32 in
Length	40 15¾	43 17	46 cm 18 in
Sleeve seam	24 9½	28 11	31 cm 12 in

TENSION
26 sts and 34 rows to 10cm/4in square over st st on 3¼mm (No 10/US 3) needles.

ABBREVIATIONS
See page 42.

BACK
With 2¾mm (No 12/US 2) needles and A, cast on 92(98:106) sts. K 7 rows.
Change to 3¼mm (No 10/US 3) needles.
1st row (right side): With B, K to end.
2nd row: With B, K5, P to last 5 sts, K5.
Rep last 2 rows once. Change to A and rep 1st and 2nd rows twice.
Beg with a K row, work in st st and stripe patt of 4 rows B and 4 rows A until Back measures 24(25:26)cm/9½(10:10¼)in from beg, ending with 4th row of A or B stripe.
Cont in stripe patt, work as follows:
Next row: K5, P6, K to last 11 sts, P6, K5.
Next row: P. **
Rep last 2 rows until Back measures 40(43:46)cm/15¾(17:18)in from beg, ending with a wrong side row.
Shape Shoulders
Cast off 24(26:29) sts at beg of next 2 rows. Cast off rem 44(46:48) sts.

FRONT
Work as given for Back to **. Rep last 2 rows until Front measures 34(37:39)cm/13½(14¾:15¼)in from beg, ending with a wrong side row.
Shape Neck
Next row: Patt 37(39:42), cast off next 18(20:22) sts, patt to end.
Work on last set of sts only. Dec 1 st at neck edge on next 10 rows, then on 3 foll alt rows [24(26:29) sts]. Cont straight for a few rows until Front matches Back to shoulder shaping, ending at side edge. Cast off.
With wrong side of work facing, rejoin yarn to rem sts and patt to end. Complete to match first side.

SLEEVES
With 2¾mm (No 12/US 2) needles and A, cast on 38(42:42) sts.
1st row (right side): With A, K2, [P2, K2] to end.
2nd row: With A, P2, [K2, P2] to end.
Rep last 2 rows once more. Change to B and rep 1st and 2nd rows twice.
Rep last 8 rows once more inc 6(4:6) sts evenly across last row [44(46:48) sts].
Change to 3¼mm (No 10/US 3) needles.
Beg with a K row, work in st st and stripe patt as before, inc 1 st at each end of every 2nd(2nd:3rd) row until there are 64(66:92) sts, then on every foll 3rd(3rd:4th) row until there are 90(94:98) sts. Cont straight until Sleeve measures 24(28:31)cm/9½(11:12)in from beg, ending with a wrong side row. Cast off.

HOOD
With 3¼mm (No 10/US 3) needles and A, cast on 47(51:55) sts.
1st row (right side): With A, K to end.
2nd row: With A, K5, P to end.
Rep last 2 rows once more. Change to B and rep 1st and 2nd rows twice.
Rep last 8 rows until Hood measures approximately 46(51:55)cm/18(20:21½)in from beg, ending with 4th row of A stripe.
Cast off with A.

TO MAKE UP
Join shoulder seams. Sew on sleeves, placing centre of sleeves to shoulder seams. Beginning 4cm/1½in from cast on edge, join side seams, then sleeve seams. Fold hood in half lengthwise and join back seam. Sew hood in place.

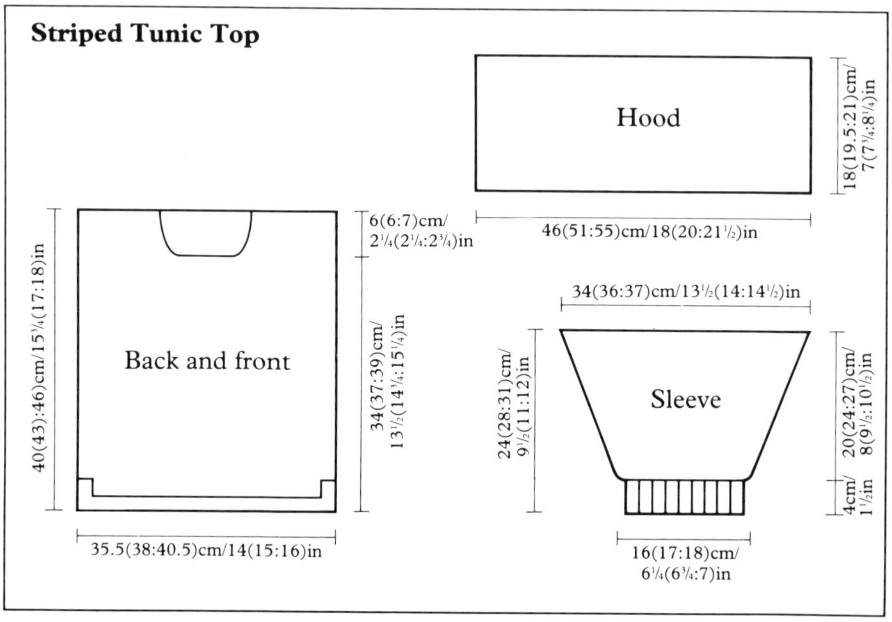
Striped Tunic Top
Hood
18(19.5:21)cm/ 7(7¾:8¼)in
46(51:55)cm/18(20:21½)in
6(6:7)cm/ 2¼(2¼:2¾)in
40(43):46)cm/15¾(17:18)in
Back and front
34(37:39)cm/ 13½(14¾:15¼)in
35.5(38:40.5)cm/14(15:16)in
34(36:37)cm/13½(14:14½)in
24(28:31)cm/ 9½(11:12)in
Sleeve
20(24:27)cm/ 8(9½:10½)in
4cm/ 1½in
16(17:18)cm/ 6¼(6¾:7)in

Sampler Sweater page 38

MATERIALS

9 50g balls of Rowan DK Handknit Cotton.
Pair each of 3¼mm (No 10/US 3) and 4mm (No 8/US 6) knitting needles.
One 3¼mm (No 10/US 3) circular knitting needle, 40cm/16in long.
Cable needle.

MEASUREMENTS

To fit age	2–3 years
Actual chest measurement	76 cm 30 in
Length	42 cm 16½in
Sleeve seam	24 cm 9½in

TENSION

20 sts and 28 rows to 10cm/4in square over st st on 4mm (No 8/US 6) needles.

ABBREVIATIONS

MB = K into front, back and front of next st, turn, P3, turn, sl 1, K2 tog, psso.
Also see page 42.

PANEL A

Worked over 10 sts.
1st row (right side): P1, K1, P1, K4, P1, K1, P1.
2nd row: P1, K1, P6, K1, P1.
3rd row: P1, K1, P1, sl next 2 sts onto cable needle and leave at front of work, K2, then K2 from cable needle, P1, K1, P1.
4th row: As 2nd row.
These 4 rows form patt.

MOTIF B

Worked over 15 sts.
1st row (right side): K1, P13, K1.
2nd row: P1, K13, P1.
3rd row: As 1st row.
4th row and every foll alt row: P15.
5th row: K15.
7th row: K7, MB, K7.
9th row: K5, MB, K3, MB, K5.
11th row: K4, MB, K5, MB, K4.
13th row: K3, MB, K7, MB, K3.
15th row: K3, [MB, K3] 3 times.
17th row: As 9th row.
19th row: K15.
20th row: P15.

MOTIF C

Worked over 15 sts.
1st row (right side): K1, P13, K1.
2nd row: P1, K13, P1.
3rd row: As 1st row.
4th row: P15.
5th row: K15.
6th row: P15.
7th row: K7, P1, K7.
8th row: P6, K1, P1, K1, P6.
9th row: K5, P1, [K1, P1] twice, K5.
10th row: P4, K1, [P1, K1] 3 times, P4.
11th row: K3, P1, [K1, P1] 4 times, K3.
12th row: P2, K1, [P1, K1] 5 times, P2.
13th row: As 11th row.
14th row: As 10th row.
15th row: As 9th row.
16th row: As 8th row.
17th row: As 7th row.
18th to 20th rows: As 4th to 6th rows.

MOTIF D

Worked over 15 sts.
1st row (right side): K1, P13, K1.
2nd row: P1, K13, P1.
3rd row: As 1st row.
4th row: P15.
5th row: K7, P1, K7.
6th row: P6, K1, P1, K1, P6.
7th row: K5, P1, K3, P1, K5.
8th row: P4, K1, [P2, K1] twice, P4.
9th row: K3, P1, K2, P1, K1, P1, K2, P1, K3.
10th row: [P2, K1] twice, P3, [K1, P2] twice.
11th row: K4, P1, [K2, P1] twice, K4.
12th row: P3, K1, P2, K1, P1, K1, P2, K1, P3.
13th row: As 7th row.
14th row: As 8th row.
15th row: K6, P1, K1, P1, K6.
16th row: P5, K1, P3, K1, P5.
17th and 18th rows: As 5th and 6th rows.
19th row: As 5th row.
20th row: P15.

MOTIF E

Worked over 15 sts.
1st row (right side): K1, P13, K1.
2nd row: P1, K13, P1.
3rd row: As 1st row.
4th row and every foll alt row: P15.
5th row: K15.
7th row: K5, K2 tog, yf, K1, yf, skpo, K5.
9th row: K4, K2 tog, yf, K3, yf, skpo, K4.
11th row: K3, K2 tog, yf, K2, K into front, back and front of next st, turn, P3, turn, K3, turn, P1, P2 tog, turn, K2 tog, K2, yf, skpo, K3.
13th row: K4, yf, skpo, K3, K2 tog, yf, K4.
15th row: K5, yf, skpo, K1, K2 tog, yf, K5.
17th row: K6, yf, sl 1, K2 tog, psso, yf, K6.
19th row: K15.
20th row: P15.

BACK

With 3¼mm (No 10/US 3) needles cast on 82 sts.
1st row (right side): K2, [P2, K2] to end.
2nd row: P2, [K2, P2] to end.
Rep last 2 rows 5 times more, inc 3 sts evenly across last row [85 sts].
Change to 4mm (No 8/US 6) needles.
Beg with a K row, work 18 rows in st st.

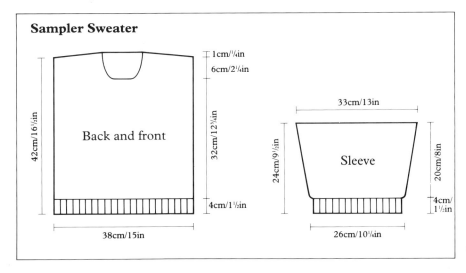

Sampler Sweater

Back and front — 42cm/16½in, 32cm/12¾in, 38cm/15in, 4cm/1½in, 1cm/¼in, 6cm/2¼in

Sleeve — 33cm/13in, 24cm/9½in, 20cm/8in, 26cm/10¼in, 4cm/1½in

Work patt as follows:

1st row (right side): * Work 1st row of Panel A, Motif B and Panel A *; work 1st row of Motif C, rep from * to *.

Work a further 19 rows as set.

21st row: * Work 1st row of Panel A, Motif D and Panel A *; work 1st row of Motif E, rep from * to *.

Work a further 19 rows as set.

The last 40 rows form patt. ** Rep last 40 rows once more, then work first 20 rows again.

Shape Shoulders

Keeping patt correct, cast off 13 sts at beg of next 4 rows. Leave rem 33 sts on a holder.

FRONT

Work as given for Back to **. Rep last 40 rows once more.

Shape Neck

Next row: Patt 35, turn.

Work on this set of sts only. Keeping patt correct, dec 1 st at neck edge on every row until 26 sts rem. Cont straight until Front matches Back to shoulder shaping, ending at side edge.

Shape Shoulders

Cast off 13 sts at beg of next row. Work 1 row. Cast off rem 13 sts.

With right side facing, slip centre 15 sts onto a holder, rejoin yarn to rem sts and patt to end. Complete to match first side.

SLEEVES

With 3¼mm (No 10/US 3) needles cast on 34 sts.

Work 11 rows in rib as given for Back welt.

Inc row: Rib 2, [inc in next st, rib 4] 6 times, inc in next st, rib 1 [41 sts].

Change to 4mm (No 8/US 6) needles. Beg with a K row, work 18 rows in st st, inc 1 st at each end of every 3rd row [53 sts].

Work patt as follows:

1st row (right side): P8, K1, work 1st row of Panel A, Motif C and Panel A, K1, P8.

2nd row: K8, P1, work 2nd row of Panel A, Motif C and Panel A, P1, K8.

These 2 rows set position of patt. Cont as set, matching patt to Back, **at the same time**, inc 1 st at each end of next row and every foll 3rd row until there are 71 sts, working inc sts into patt. Work a further 16 rows straight. Cast off.

COLLAR

Join shoulder seams.

With right side facing, sl first 7 sts from centre of front neck onto a safety pin,

rejoin yarn and with 3¼mm (No 10/US 3) circular needle, K rem 8 sts, then pick up and K19 sts up right front neck, K across centre back neck sts, dec 3 sts evenly over each Panel A sts, pick up and K19 sts down left front neck, then K7 sts from safety pin [80 sts]. Work 4 rounds in P1, K1 rib.

Turn and work backwards and forwards as follows:

Next row: K1, P1, M1, [P1, K1] 12 times, * [P1, K1] twice, M1, [K1, P1] twice, M1; rep from * twice more, [P1, K1] to end [87 sts].

Next row: K1, P1, M1, K1, [P1, K1] to last 2 sts, M1, P1, K1.

Next row: K1, P2, K1, [P1, K1] to last 3 sts, P2, K1.

Next row: K1, P1, M1, P1, [K1, P1] to last 2 sts, M1, P1, K1.

Next row: K1, [P1, K1] to end.

Rep last 4 rows 5 times more, then work the first 2 rows of the 4 rows again. Cast off loosely in patt.

TO MAKE UP

Sew on sleeves, placing centre of sleeves to shoulder seams. Join side and sleeve seams.

Aran Sweater with Sailor Collar and Striped Inset page 39

MATERIALS

10(11) 50g balls of Rowan DK Handknit Cotton in Blue (MC).

1 50g ball of same in White (A).

Pair each of 3¼mm (No 10/US 3) and 4mm (No 8/US 6) knitting needles.

Cable needle.

MEASUREMENTS

To fit age	2–3	3–4 years
Actual chest measurement	70 27½	74 cm 29 in
Length	42 16½	45 cm 17¾ in
Sleeve seam	25 10	30 cm 11¾ in

TENSION

20 sts and 28 rows to 10cm/4in square over st st on 4mm (No 8/US 6) needles.

ABBREVIATIONS

C4B = sl next 2 sts onto cable needle and leave at back of work, K2, then K2 from cable needle;

C4F = sl next 2 sts onto cable needle and leave at front of work, K2, then K2 from cable needle;

Cr2L = sl next st onto cable needle and leave at front of work, P1, then K st from cable needle;

Cr2R = sl next st onto cable needle and leave at back of work, K1, then P st from cable needle;

Cr3L = sl next 2 sts onto cable needle and leave at front of work, P1, then K2 from cable needle;

Cr3R = sl next st onto cable needle and leave at back of work, K2, then P st from cable needle.

Also see page 42.

PANEL A

Worked over 8 sts.

1st row and every foll alt row (wrong side): P8.

2nd row: K8.

4th row: C4B, C4F.

6th row: K8.

8th row: C4F, C4B.

10th row: K8.

12th row: C4F, C4B.

14th row: K8.

16th row: C4B, C4F.

These 16 rows form patt.

PANEL B

Worked over 16 sts.

1st row (wrong side): K6, P4, K6.

2nd row: P6, C4F, P6.

3rd row: As 1st row.

4th row: P5, Cr3R, Cr3L, P5.

5th row: K5, P2, K2, P2, K5.

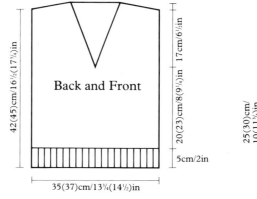

Aran Sweater with Sailor Collar and Striped Inset

Back and Front
42(45)cm/16½(17¾)in
20(23)cm/8(9¼)in
17cm/6½in
5cm/2in
35(37)cm/13¼(14½)in

Sleeve
33(34)cm/13(13½)in
25(30)cm/10(11¾)in
20(25)cm/8(9¾)in
5cm/2in
24cm/9½in

6th row: P4, Cr3R, P2, Cr3L, P4.
7th row: K4, [P2, K4] twice.
8th row: P3, Cr3R, P4, Cr3L, P3.
9th row: K3, P2, K6, P2, K3.
10th row: P2, [Cr3R] twice, [Cr3L] twice, P2.
11th row: K2, [P2, K1, P2, K2] twice.
12th row: P1, [Cr3R] twice, P2, [Cr3L] twice, P1.
13th row: [K1, P2] twice, K4, [P2, K1] twice.
14th row: P1, K1, Cr2L, Cr3L, P2, Cr3R, Cr2R, K1, P1.
15th row: [K1, P1] twice, K1, P2, K2, P2, K1, [P1, K1] twice.
16th row: P1, K1, P1, Cr2L, Cr3L, Cr3R, Cr2R, P1, K1, P1.
17th row: K1, P1, K2, P1, K1, P4, K1, P1, K2, P1, K1.
18th row: P1, Cr2L, Cr2R, P1, C4F, P1, Cr2L, Cr2R, P1.
19th row: K2, P2, K2, P4, K2, P2, K2.
Rows 4th to 19th form patt.

BACK

With 3¼mm (No 10/US 3) needles and MC, cast on 74(80) sts.
1st row (wrong side): K2, [P1 tbl, K2] 3(4) times, * P4, K2, [P1 tbl, K2] 3 times, P4 *; K2, [P1 tbl, K2] 4 times, rep from * to *, K2, [P1 tbl, K2] 3(4) times.
2nd row: P2, [K1 tbl, P2] 3(4) times, C4F, P2, [K1 tbl, P2] 3 times, C4F, P2, [K1 tbl, P2] 4 times, C4B, P2, [K1 tbl, P2] 3 times, C4B, P2, [K1 tbl, P2] 3(4) times.
3rd row: As 1st row.
4th row: P2, [K1 tbl, P2] 3(4) times, * K4, P2, [K1 tbl, P2] 3 times, K4 *; P2, [K1 tbl, P2] 4 times, rep from * to *, P2, [K1 tbl, P2] 3(4) times.
Rep these 4 rows twice more, then work 1st row again.
Inc row: [Patt 2(4), M1] 4(3) times, patt 12(11), M1, patt 15, M1, patt 4, M1, patt 15, M1, patt 12(11), [M1, patt 2(4)] 4(3) times [86(90) sts].
Change to 4mm (No 8/US 6) needles.
Work main patt as follows:
1st row (wrong side): [K1, P1] 6(7) times, K3, * P4, K2, work 1st row of Panel A, K2, P4 *; work 1st row of Panel B, rep from * to *, K3, [P1, K1] 6(7) times.
2nd row: [P1, K1] 6(7) times, P3, * K4, P2, work 2nd row of Panel A, P2, K4 *; work 2nd row of Panel B, rep from * to *, P3, [K1, P1] 6(7) times.
3rd row: P1, [K1, P1] 6(7) times, K2, * P4, K2, work 3rd row of Panel A, K2, P4 *; work 3rd row of Panel B, rep from * to *, K2, [P1, K1] 6(7) times, P1.
4th row: K1, [P1, K1] 6(7) times, P2, C4F, P2, work 4th row of Panel A, P2, C4F, work 4th row of Panel B, C4B, P2, work 4th row of Panel A, P2, C4B, P2, [K1, P1] 6(7) times, K1.
These 4 rows set position of Panels and form double moss st patt at side edges.
Cont in patt as set until work measures 42(45)cm/16½(17¾)in from beg, ending with a wrong side row.
Shape Shoulders
Cast off 10(11) sts at beg of next 2 rows and 11 sts at beg of foll 2 rows. Cast off rem 44(46) sts.

FRONT

Work as given for Back until Front measures 25(28)cm/10(11¼)in from beg, ending with a wrong side row.
Shape Neck
Next row: Patt 43(45), turn.
Work on this set of sts only. Keeping patt correct, dec 1 st at neck edge on every foll

alt row until 21(22) sts rem. Cont straight until Front matches Back to shoulder shaping, ending at side edge.
Shape Shoulders
Cast off 10(11) sts at beg of next row.
Work 1 row. Cast off rem 11 sts.
With right side facing, rejoin yarn to rem sts and patt to end. Complete to match first side.

SLEEVES

With 3¼mm (No 10/US 3) needles and MC, cast on 50 sts.
1st row (wrong side): K2, [P1 tbl, K2] 4 times, * P4, K2, [P1 tbl, K2] 4 times; rep from * once more.
2nd row: P2, [K1 tbl, P2] 4 times, C4F, P2, [K1 tbl, P2] 4 times, C4B, P2, [K1 tbl, P2] 4 times.
3rd row: As 1st row.
4th row: P2, [K1 tbl, P2] 4 times, * K4, P2, [K1 tbl, P2] 4 times; rep from * once more.
Rep these 4 rows twice more, then work 1st row again.
Inc row: [Patt 2, M1] 6 times, patt 11, ML, patt 4, ML, patt 11, [M1, patt 2] 6 times [64 sts].
Change to 4mm (No 8/US 6) needles.
Work main patt as follows:
1st row (wrong side): P1, K3, * P4, K2, work 1st row of Panel A, K2, P4 *; work 1st row of Panel B, rep from * to *, K3, P1.
2nd row: K1, P3, * K4, P2, work 2nd row of Panel A, P2, K4 *; work 2nd row of Panel B, rep from * to *, P3, K1.
3rd row: K1, P1, K2, * P4, K2, work 3rd row of Panel A, K2, P4 *; work 3rd row of Panel B, rep from * to *, K2, P1, K1.
4th row: P1, K1, P2, C4F, P2, work 4th row of Panel A, P2, C4F, work 4th row of Panel B, C4B, P2, work 4th row of Panel A, P2, C4B, P2, K1, P1.
These 4 rows set position of Panels and form double moss st at side edges.
Cont in patt as set, **at the same time**, inc 1 st at each end of next row and every foll 6th(7th) row until there are 78(82) sts, work inc sts into double moss st patt. Cont straight until Sleeve measures 25(30)cm/10(11¾)in from beg, ending with a wrong side row. Cast off.

COLLAR

With 3¼mm (No 10/US 3) needles and MC, cast on 83(86) sts.
1st row (wrong side): K2, [P1 tbl, K2] to end.
2nd row: P2, [K1 tbl, P2] to end.
Work a further 3 rows, dec 1 st at each end of next row and foll alt row.
Next row: Work 2 tog, rib 3(8), [M1, rib 8(7)] to last 2 sts, work 2 tog [86(90) sts].
Change to 4mm (No 8/US 6) needles.
Work in main patt as given for Back until Collar measures 17(19)cm/6¾(7¼)in from beg, ending with a wrong side row.
Shape Neck
Next row: Patt 33, cast off next 20(24) sts, patt to end.
Work on last set of sts only for left side of front collar. Patt 1 row.
Cast off 3 sts at beg of next row and foll alt row. Dec 1 st at inside edge on every right side row until 20 sts rem, then on every row until 2 sts rem. Work 2 tog and fasten off.
With wrong side facing, rejoin yarn to rem sts and patt 2 rows. Complete to match left side.

COLLAR EDGINGS

With 3¼mm (No 10/US 3) needles, MC and right side facing, pick up and K62(65) sts evenly along one outside edge of collar omitting rib. Beg with a 1st row, work 5 rows in rib as given for Collar, inc 1 st at each end of every alt row. Cast off in rib. Work other side in same way.

INSET

With 4mm (No 8/US 6) needles and MC, cast on 3 sts.
Beg with a K row, work in st st and stripe patt of 4 rows MC and 4 rows A, **at the same time**, inc 1 st at each end of every alt row until there are 31 sts, ending with 4th row of MC stripe.
Cont in MC only. P 1 row for fold line.
Beg with a P row, work 3 rows in st st, dec 1 st at each end of 1st and 3rd rows. Cast off.

TO MAKE UP

Join shoulder seams. Sew on sleeves, placing centre of sleeves to shoulder seams. Join side and sleeve seams. Mitre corners of collar edgings, then sew collar in place. Fold top of inset at fold line to wrong side and slip stitch in position. Sew in inset.

Author's Acknowledgements

I would like to thank the following for their invaluable help: Gisela Blum, Pat Church, Berenice Hazle, Joan Holcombe, Penny Hill, Maisie Lawrence, Frances Wallace and Betty Webb.

I am especially grateful to Tina Egleton for her pattern checking, technical expertise and unfailing patience, Pia Tryde for her wonderful photography, Marie Willey for her perfect styling, Jane Donovan and Carey Smith for their commitment to the project, and, as always, Heather Jeeves, my agent, for her continued support.

I would also like to thank the following children, and their mums and dads for their patience and good humour: Danielle, Emma, Eleanor, Georgia, Graham, Hannah, Imogen, James, Jennifer, Karah, Lewis, Lucy, Melina, Montana, Nancy, Nicholas, Nicola, Nicoli, Oliver, Stevie and William.

ROWAN YARNS ADDRESSES

Rowan yarns can be obtained from stockists of good quality knitting yarns. In case of difficulty in obtaining yarns, write to the addresses below for a list of stockists in your area.

U.K.: Rowan Yarns, Green Lane Mill, Holmfirth, West Yorkshire, England HD7 1RW.
Tel: (0484) 681881

U.S.A.: Westminster Trading Corporation, 5 Northern Boulevard, Amherst, NH 03031.
Tel: (603) 886 5041/5043

Australia: Rowan (Australia), 191 Canterbury Road, Canterbury, Victoria 3126.
Tel: (03) 830 1609

Belgium: Hedera, Pleinstraat 68, 3001 Leuven.
Tel: (016) 23 21 89

Canada: Estelle Designs & Sales Ltd, Units 65/67, 2220 Midland Avenue, Scarborough, Ontario M1P 3E6.
Tel: (416) 298 9922

Denmark: Designer Garn, Vesterbro 33A, DK-9000 Aalborg.
Tel: 98 13 48 24

Finland: Helmi Vuorelma-Oy, Vesijarvenkatu 13, SF-15141 Lahti.
Tel: (018) 826 831

France: Sidel, Ch. Depart. 14C, 13840 Rognes.
Tel: (33) 42 50 15 06

Germany: Christoph Fritzsch GmbH, Gewerbepark Dogelmuhle, D-6367 Karben 1.
Tel: 06039 2071

Holland: Henk & Henrietta Beukers, Dorpsstraat 9, NL 5327 AR Hurwenen.
Tel: 04182 1764

Iceland: Stockurinn, Kjorgardi, Laugavegi 59, ICE-101 Reykjavik.
Tel: (01) 18258

Italy: La Compagnia del Cotone, Via Mazzini 44, I-10123 Torino.
Tel: (011) 87 83 81

Japan: Diakeito Co Ltd, 2-3-11 Senba-Higashi, Minoh City, Osaka 562.
Tel: 0727 27 6604

Mexico: Rebecca Pick Estambresy Tejidos Finos S.A. de C.V., A.V. Michoacan 30-A, Local 3 Esq Av Mexico, Col Hipodromo Condesa 06170, Mexico 11.
Tel: (05) 2 64 84 74

New Zealand: John Q Goldingham Ltd, PO Box 45083, Epuni Railway, Lower Hutt.
Tel: (04) 5674 085

Norway: Eureka, PO Box 357, N-1401 Ski.
Tel: 64 86 55 40

Sweden: Wincent, Sveavagen 94, 113 50 Stockholm.
Tel: (08) 673 70 60